New Library of Pastoral Care
GENERAL EDITOR: DEREK BLOWS

STILL SMALL VOICE

*A Practical Introduction to Counselling
for Pastors and Other Helpers*

Michael Jacobs

First published 1982
SPCK
Holy Trinity Church
Marylebone Road
London NW1 4DU

Eighth impression 1990

ISBN 0 281 03852 X

Filmset by Pioneer
Printed and bound in Great Britain by
Courier International Ltd, Tiptree, Essex

Contents

Foreword

The *New Library of Pastoral Care* has been planned to meet the needs of those people concerned with pastoral care, whether clergy or lay, who seek to improve their knowledge and skills in this field. Equally, it is hoped that it may prove useful to those secular helpers who may wish to understand the role of the pastor.

Pastoral care in every age has drawn from contemporary secular knowledge to inform its understanding of man and his various needs and of the ways in which these needs might be met. Today it is perhaps the secular helping professions of social work, counselling and psychotherapy, and community development which have particular contributions to make to the pastor in his work. Such knowledge does not stand still, and pastors would have a struggle to keep up with the endless tide of new developments which pour out from these and other disciplines, and to sort out which ideas and practices might be relevant to his particular pastoral needs. Among present-day ideas, for instance, of particular value might be an understanding of the social context of the pastoral task, the dynamics of the helping relationship, the attitudes and skills as well as factual knowledge which might make for effective pastoral intervention, and perhaps most significant of all, the study of particular cases, whether through verbatim reports of interviews or general case presentation. The discovery of ways of learning from what one is doing is becoming increasingly important.

There is always a danger that a pastor who drinks deeply at the well of a secular discipline may lose his grasp of his own pastoral identity and become 'just another' social worker or counsellor. It in no way detracts from the value of these professions to assert that the role and task of the pastor are quite unique among the helping professions and deserve to be clarified and strengthened rather than weakened. The theological commitment of the pastor and the appropriate use of his role will be a recurrent theme of the series. At the same time the pastor cannot afford to work in a vacuum. He needs to be able to communicate and co-operate with those helpers in other disciplines whose work may overlap, without loss of his own unique role. This in turn will mean being able to communicate with them through some understanding of their concepts and language.

Finally, there is a rich variety of styles and approaches in pastoral work within the various religious traditions. No attempt will be made to secure a uniform approach. The Library will contain the variety, and even perhaps occasional eccentricity, which such a title suggests. Some books will be more specifically theological and others more concerned with particular areas of need or practice. It is hoped that all of them will have a usefulness that will reach right across the boundaries of religious denomination.

DEREK BLOWS
Series Editor

Preface

When SPCK approached me to write a book on pastoral counselling, it was a happy coincidence that mention was made of building upon R.S. Lee's *Principles of Pastoral Counselling* for an introductory volume for the New Library of Pastoral Care. It was Roy Lee whom I was advised to meet in 1967 when I was considering a psychological study of an English mystic. He promptly advised me to read Freud, and not Jung, who up to that point had fascinated me. Although we met only once, he started me on a personal and professional pilgrimage through Freud and post-Freud, which led from reading to practice under supervision, more formal training and personal therapy, and to a full-time post in counselling and psychotherapy. In recent years this work has expanded into the training of professional and voluntary 'care-givers' in counselling methods and theory. The work on the mystic got no further, and I have moved a long way since then. But I am glad to be able to continue that lead given to me (and others) by Roy Lee.

Since this book is itself an introduction, it needs little introducing. I should say that many of my references to both counsellors and clients appear to confine them to the masculine gender. It scarcely needs saying that this is a convenient literary device, and that as far as I am concerned I do not confine the ministry (priestly or otherwise) to men. I should also point out that I have disguised the details of every example I have used, because I would have no wish that those who have helped me to learn should identify themselves. There is one exception, which though disguised could have led to recognition, and I am grateful to that person for her permission to use her counselling as an example of what can be achieved.

There are so many people who have taught, guided, influenced and sustained me that to list them would bore the reader, and would probably lead to someone being missed. Those who know me can rest assured of my thanks. Fellow-members of the Association for Pastoral Care and Counselling, the British Association for Counselling, and the Student Health Service in Leicester have been foremost in my personal and professional development over the last ten years. Three people in particular I do wish to single out for my thanks and to crave their indulgence: Jimmy Crighton, who trusted me as an inexperienced counsellor with a post in his team, and who will now sometimes wonder whether he has gained a counsellor who spends too much time teaching and writing; Isobel Hunter-Brown, who has taught me so much in supervision, and who will I hope forgive the errors in analytic technique which have crept into this book; and Doreen Schofield who has a way of helping me cut through jargon and verbiage, but who will have to forgive my constant use of terms like 'exploration'. They have been valued colleagues.

I am also grateful to Mrs Florence Townsend for typing this and other manuscripts for me. Above all, it is difficult to thank enough my wife Valerie, and our three children Mary, Andrew and Susanna, both for their tolerance of a frequently absent husband and father on counselling business, and latterly at the typewriter, and for the secure and loving environment they create at home. Without their support I doubt whether I would have survived intact the early, painful years of learning, and I would be the poorer now both as a person and as a counsellor.

Michael Jacobs
Leicester 1981

PART ONE
Pastoral Counselling in Context

ONE

Different Perspectives

Alan approached his school chaplain after chapel and asked
to see him. They arranged to meet when the chaplain knew
they would have time to talk. When Alan came he rather
hesitantly asked if he was permitted to take communion if
he did not believe in the resurrection of the body.

'What do you think about Christ's resurrection, Alan?'

'I can't believe his actual physical body rose from the
dead. When the gospels were written people thought
differently, not as we do today. I don't know what to
believe, but I guess it stands for something. But the Bible
says it's true, and I mustn't contradict the Gospels.'

'What you're saying isn't all that different from some of
the theologians writing today. Do you think you have to
take the Bible literally?'

'I don't like to question things like the Bible — it's got
God's authority behind it.'

'And you don't like to question authority?'

'I guess I don't. My dad always knows what he wants for
me, and I find it difficult to disagree with him . . .'

And the conversation went on. The chaplain knew,
because he tried to keep his finger on the pulse of the life of
the school, that Alan was worrying about his A-levels, and
guessed that his father might be putting pressure on his
son because he wanted him to get into Oxbridge. That
conversation began a series of meetings in which Alan was
helped, among other things, to contain his anxieties which
were building up about the exams. Lest it be thought that
his original question was forgotten (which in the first
instance it was) Alan eventually took his own decision and
received communion.

Or take a different setting:
After an evening class on Christian Ethics, Miss Berridge
approached the lecturer. 'I wonder if you could give me
some advice. The friend I live with is drinking a lot, and I
think she might become an alcoholic. Where can she get
some help?' The room was now empty, and the lecturer
could see that Miss Berridge looked tearful.
    'You're obviously worried. Is her drinking upsetting you?'
    She burst into tears. 'Yes, you see I think I'm drinking
too much as well. I'm afraid I might be an alcoholic.'
    The lecturer allowed her time to calm down, and then
asked her whether she would like to meet at a later time
and talk about her worries. Miss Berridge, with considerable relief, agreed.

The chaplain or the lecturer in either of these situations could
simply have answered the question. But neither chose to.
Because each had some experience in counselling, and
sufficient sensitivity to realize that it was more than
information that was being asked for, each was able to draw
out areas of concern in the troubled person, which eventually
led to a deeper exploration of the questions originally asked.
    There are, of course, many ways in which a pastor (or any
other person involved in a caring capacity) could have
answered either of these two people. The chaplain might, for
instance, have taken the opportunity to spell out the Christian
belief in the resurrection of the body, and might have gone on
to insist (depending on his own convictions) that to receive
communion when not accepting the Creed was not per-
missible. A more liberal theologian might have discussed
Alan's ideas with him, explaining perhaps some of Bultmann's
thinking, in an attempt to help the young man come to grips
intellectually with problems of biblical and historical
interpretation. We could call this method didactic—it is the
teaching/preaching role of the pastor.
    A different approach would be to look at moral issues—par-
ticularly in the second example. Building on the setting (a
class on Christian Ethics) the lecturer might have taken the
chance to examine the moral dilemma. Had it been a parish
setting, a pastor might have encouraged Miss Berridge to give
up, or moderate, her drinking, and advised her to pray for

strength to do so. We could call this approach exhortatory.

Alternatively, in certain traditions a priest might suggest that a person consider confession, assuring that God's forgiveness awaits the person who acknowledges guilt. Confession might bring relief to the troubled person, while the forgiveness mediated through the priest might help the person to start life afresh. The confessional model certainly provides a sense of release to some, and conveys, in the acceptance of the priest, new strength which might alter the situation—though in such a case as this, I guess the change would be only temporary. We have therefore a third approach, the confessional.

Confession also enables the priest to give advice (when asked), although advice-giving is a model which is used extensively in other settings. We can imagine a situation in the second example where the lecturer takes Miss Berridge at face value, and simply points her to some of the resources to help alcoholics, which she could then pass on to her friend. If he was more subtle, he would spot (as indeed he did) that the friend's problem was also her problem, and he might have gone on to give her the address of someone who could help her. Many other professional helpers might have acted similarly, uneasy at dealing more directly with the person in difficulty. This model is the information- or advice-giving approach.

None of the ways already outlined are wrong. They are all examples of typical approaches to pastoral care which have been commonly used, and no doubt at times with good effect. Both the circumstances in which the pastor is asked for help, his own inclinations and his particular skills will in large measure dictate his response. In this book emphasis is given to an approach which has come to be called 'counselling'. Counselling is characterized not by active intervention, as in the approaches outlined above, but by the 'still, small voice' of my title. Stated briefly (since later chapters will spell out the approach in more detail) it is a way of helping others which stresses the gentle stillness of the helper in listening, absorbing, containing and understanding.

Counselling stresses the calm acceptance of the other— which may also apply in the other models described—but goes on from there to stress a relationship in which the helper, and what he believes, takes second place. Teaching, exhortation (whether to prayer or confession), moralizing, and advice-giving are laid aside, to encourage the 'still, small voice' which speaks in the other, although it may take some time for a person in trouble to pass through the storms inside before that voice begins to be heard. And although there can be few pastors now who, at least in pastoral care, thump the Bible, or ram the beliefs of the Church and the moral judgements of religion down others' throats, such forms of ecclesiastical 'earthquake, wind and fire' are put aside. It is not in those ways that the inner voice will be heard. It is in the stillness, the unhurried calm, the quietness (but not the quiescence) that a person who is in distress can be helped to listen more fully to himself.

Counselling (as we shall see) does not ignore the obvious, but it seeks to reach behind it. It requires the giving of sufficient time to help a person in distress to uncover and reach some of the less obvious and less acceptable feelings and thoughts which contribute to unhappiness and dissatisfaction. It is an approach which has isolated certain factors in caring relationships and stressed them, while at the same time playing down other factors such as giving answers, expressing sympathy, or actively trying to change the circumstances which appear to contribute to the distress. Again, none of these are wrong, but are less used in counselling. While a counselling approach is not appropriate for every pastoral situation, it is capable of being much more widely used. It is a way of helping which uses identifiable skills to help a person to help himself, to come to his own conclusions, and to decide in what ways he might begin to change both his circumstances and himself. It is above all an approach which tries to understand what goes on inside people, and how internal difficulties can stand in the way of change, rather than looking at external factors or external solutions.

As such counselling is one of the many skills which today's pastor has available to him in his ministry. But it is not in any sense a 'modern' skill, because counselling is not new. I would certainly be suspicious if it were seen as a 'trendy' activity.[1] When King Solomon refused to judge which of the two women was the true mother of the disputed baby, he showed insight which is typical of the counselling approach.

He appeared uncaring, and he ordered the child to be cut in two. The response which this threat evoked from the real mother showed his awareness, which we would now call 'psychological knowledge', and his refusal to judge without exploring enabled the truth to be revealed.

'Counsel' is a word with a fine theological tradition, and although some counsel has included the giving of direct advice, different societies at various times have had people who often spoke the truth obliquely, looking at familiar situations from new and challenging perspectives—amongst such people are the witch-doctor, the druid, the seer and the prophet, the hermit, the confessor and the priest, the philosopher, the alchemist and the family doctor. Even the Fool, who appears in some of Shakespeare's plays as the counsellor to those in authority, frequently demonstrates both care and wisdom in his aphorisms and his riddles. Howard Clinebell reminds us of the value of the counsellor when he prefaces his own book, *Basic Types of Pastoral Counselling* with these words from the Book of Proverbs: 'Where there is no guidance a people falls; but in an abundance of counsellors there is safety.' (Prov. 11.14)

Counselling is not an activity which is confined to professional counsellors. The British Association for Counselling rightly states in the preamble to its definition of counselling that it 'has no proprietary rights to the use of the word.'[2] Current counselling techniques have built, in many cases, upon age-old ways of caring, isolating certain features which are conducive to what has been called (I shall suggest mistakenly) the 'non-directive' approach. The term 'non-directive' may highlight at this point one of the distinctions between this set of skills and others which are also used in pastoral work.

The approach which is outlined in this book is no more nor less 'secular' than many of the other skills required of the pastor. Writing sermons requires similar skills to any other writing, and the conduct of worship, and preaching of sermons, require many of the techniques developed by the public speaker or even the actor. When I was at theological college we did not think twice about being trained in voice-production for preaching and singing. So, although there is a sense in which we can use pastoral counselling as an

expression to distinguish it from other types of counselling
(see chapter 2), the basic skills which form the substance of
this book apply to a variety of settings.

For that reason the examples used to illustrate counselling
technique are drawn from pastoral and secular settings. Just
as no Christian (who is sufficiently open-minded to this
approach) need fear that counselling undermines true faith,
so those who help people in other settings need not be
troubled that pastoral counselling is a subversive approach to
convert people to Christianity, or that what is written here is
only applicable to pastoral settings. Those who care for
others, wherever they work and whatever their beliefs, will, I
hope, find some guidance here to enrich their work. It will
become clear that the counsellor, pastoral or otherwise, is in
one sense a neutral figure in the helping relationship. But
neutral does not mean uncaring, nor impotent.

This book is not designed to make the reader into a full-
time counsellor. Like the term psychoanalysis, counselling
describes both a small professional discipline, and also a
much larger 'professional' approach to people. There are in
fact very few full-time counsellors in Britain, mainly working
in secondary or tertiary education, with a few in the National
Health Service, in industry, in counselling centres, or in
private practice. Most counselling takes place either as part
of another professional activity (clergy, nurses, social workers,
etc) or in voluntary organizations (such as Marriage Guidance,
counselling centres manned by volunteers, or in specific
'problem' groups — young people, alcoholics, homosexuals,
etc). The Church already plays as large a part in counselling
as many other professions. Not only is the Association of
Pastoral Care and Counselling one of the largest divisions of
the British Association for Counselling, but clergy and others
who place value on the 'spiritual' are well represented in
other divisions. The training of ordinands of all denominations
now includes greater emphasis on the skills necessary in
sustaining pastoral relationships, and such training is in
some cases ahead of that of other professions who have still
yet to recognize the importance of the personal in the
interaction between professional and patient/client.

I hope, therefore, that this book will encourage clergy, lay
pastors, and others who work in the field of professional or

voluntary care-giving, to respond to some of the requests for help in a broader way. Counselling skills can be used in formal and informal settings. The wider application of such skills is already being seen as relevant to the many people in caring jobs who attend courses on the application of counselling to their work. I believe, as do some psycho-therapists, that by working in more depth, and over a longer period of time with a few people, we develop ways of listening, understanding and responding which can be applied more extensively in more informal and briefer contacts with greater numbers. I may therefore at times seem to stress the formal setting. But I do so in the belief that the pastor who can work with a few people in such ways will acquire knowledge capable of use in the more informal, even apparently casual, encounters of his total ministry. It is perhaps the equivalent in pastoral work of the pioneering seminars initiated by Michael Balint, himself a psychoanalyst, who met with general practitioners to see how they might develop the opportunities given to them in their brief consultations in a busy surgery.[3]

Reference to such seminars underlines the importance of going beyond reading to the sharing of one's work with others. A book has limitations. It has to use a didactic method and can act as a guide only in an area of work in which learning from within, by listening to one's own 'still, small voice' is central. What we expect of those who come for help, the sharing of themselves, we must also expect of ourselves. This book will therefore serve its purpose better if used as part of a course in counselling skills, or at the very least as part of the coming together (perhaps only of two or three) to discuss their pastoral work. Exercises which I use in my own courses are therefore included in Appendix A, designed to help put theory into practice.

All of us who help others have much to learn about the way in which we use the opportunities given to us. Clergy and lay pastors are perhaps in a unique position as being often the only people who live and work amongst the people whom they serve. They may also be unique inasmuch as they do not have a narrowly defined role. They are not like doctors, simply experts in illness, or like solicitors expert in the law, or like marriage guidance counsellors, specialists in marital situations. They can be approached, or can approach others, on many grounds. Although there is sometimes suspicion of them for what the 'cloth' or the 'faith' represents (moralizing, judgement, sin, conversion), they have opportunities often denied to others who have apparently narrower roles.

Clergy and lay pastors—'street wardens', stewards, elders —have these opportunities in an age which is becoming more sophisticated about the importance of the emotions and of other matters 'psychological'. There are signs of a backlash against the widespread use of drugs to control uncomfortable feelings, and there is some recognition that material help is not enough. Even the phrase 'it's psychological' is heard more frequently, although often as a rather glib explanation rather than as a desire to understand what this means in personal terms. 'Relationship' is a term which is in danger of becoming jargon in some quarters, but it nevertheless indicates a growing awareness that problems of living with others frequently lie at the root of much physical and emotional ill-health. Problem pages in newspapers have always been popular, but phone-ins on local radio networks, and even drama series on marriage guidance, Samaritans, and life in a mental hospital do more than appeal to the voyeuristic needs and vicarious identification of listeners and viewers with others who have problems. What were once technical psychological terms have filtered into everyday conversations and self-descriptions—introvert, extravert, neurotic, identity crisis, male menopause, etc. Although in itself this phenomenon does not necessarily indicate deeper psychological or personal awareness, popular culture is providing a base from which the counselling-minded professional or voluntary helper can work.

It is not difficult to imagine the many situations in which counselling skills and knowledge of human development can be applied in the parish or in other settings. Life-crises—the birth of a baby, problems with children, choices about education and careers, teenager/parent conflicts, marriage, moving, unemployment and redundancy, illness, retirement, old age, dying, bereavement—are occasions when a pastor might be asked directly for help, or which may be referred to in conversation, providing an opening for listening. We shall see that there are different counselling approaches—some of which are content to support, shoulder, contain and strengthen in a crisis, while others also try to uncover less obvious but equally painful feelings. The pastor is also in a position to identify those people who are in difficulty, and who need more specialized help than he can give. His intervention may make the path to such specialized help smoother.

Personal crises, alien though they are for the person experiencing them, can be creative, since the adaptation that has to take place to new circumstances involves the questioning of assumptions, particularly in relation to oneself and others. Confusion can become plasticity, from which a renewed identity emerges. Personal crises are, as the eschatology of Old and New Testaments recognizes, opportunities for growth and development. Frequently, given the help of others, they can lead to new goals and standards, based upon personal decision and not upon the rules laid down by others. After the earthquake, wind and fire of emotional turbulence, the 'still, small voice' may be heard. The personal crisis may also be a time when the 'meaning' of life (a clichéd phrase, but no less important for all that) comes under scrutiny. Here especially there is a place for pastoral counselling.

What is described in this book is one of the tools available to the pastor. It is not a substitute for caring, nor is it the only set of skills which the pastor will wish to acquire. But it has a wider application in all pastoral care, and therefore is a fitting general introduction to a series which will cover in more detail specific pastoral situations.

Notes

1. See my warning to this effect in the introduction to my paper 'Optimism and Pessimism in the Theory and Practice of Therapy and Counselling', *BAC Occasional Paper*, 1980 (see note 2).
2. *Counselling—A Definition* published by the British Association for Counselling, 1979; obtainable from 37a Sheep Street, Rugby, CV21 3BX.
3. *The Doctor, the Patient and the Illness* by Michael Balint. Pitman Medical (paperback) 1968.

TWO

Definitions and Distinctions

Since pastoral counselling, in respect of technique, draws upon more general counselling methods, any definition of its distinctiveness must begin with a brief description of the distinctions between forms of therapy and counselling. The history of psychotherapy and counselling in the twentieth century is complicated by many splits and divisions, and some models of counselling today differ widely from each other. Since the history is not essential to practice, it is described in Appendix B, which provides a background to some of the more pertinent differences with which this chapter deals.

The counselling model which is followed in this book is basically analytic (stemming from the work of Freud, Jung and their followers). Although devotees of Carl Rogers will find reference to his work, my own opinion is that his technique is most valuable in the fundamental listening and relating which lies at the heart of counselling, but that much counselling needs to go beyond his apparently 'simple' approach. I believe that he himself goes beyond what he actually writes, as I shall suggest at various points. Where the approach outlined here differs from some of the 'American' therapies (Encounter, Gestalt, psycho-drama, and some forms of co-counselling, etc) and from behaviour therapy is my emphasis on the 'still, small voice' of the counsellor, appealing to the 'still, small voice' of the person to whom he listens. It is a method of counselling which avoids even therapeutic instructions, and which does not set out to create situations deliberately aimed at evoking the catharsis of pent-up emotions. Counselling can be a slow process, and cannot be fitted into weekend workshops. It involves calmly waiting, silently opening gates, gently guiding a person into new ways of seeing and of expression. The appropriate New Testament image is that of the shepherd and the sheep, rather than driving the money-lenders like cattle out of the temple. Expressed in ecclesiastical terms, I am no believer in hard-sell evangelism (which some of the American therapies appear close to), but of the slow process of change, encouraging the frightened person to come closer to the feared parts of himself.

To call this an analytic model may engender as much suspicion as if I had espoused trans-atlantic terminology and methods. Mention of Freud may have already caused some readers to close the covers. Was not Freud anti-religion? Did he not say that belief in God is part of the universal neurosis of mankind? Is not God the projection of our needs for a super parent figure to protect us against fears of the immensity of the universe? I have no wish to embark on a far from simple debate in a book concerned with practical matters of counselling. Others have devoted more thought than I have to the theological and psychological implications of psycho-analysis and theology.[1] It has been suggested that Freud's anthropological studies, in which he makes his strongest attacks on religion, are somewhat fanciful.[2] Writing as I do from a practical point of view, I would draw attention at this stage to three points to allay some of the fears which mention of Freud and an analytic model may arouse:

Firstly, Freud has much to teach us about the structure of personality which can be separated from what he says about religion. We should not throw out the wheat (particularly his writing on technique) with the tares (the sometimes sweeping statements of psychoanalytic hypothesis).

Secondly, Freud, like other writers including those who write from within the Church, validly criticizes some attitudes which seem to accompany Christian belief. As Roy Lee writes in *Freud and Christianity*: 'If psychoanalysis helps to clear away the rubbish that clings to Christianity and frees it to grow to its full strength and maturity, it will do it an immeasurable service. If Christianity insists on clinging to neurotic manifestations of the unconscious as true religion for full-grown men and women it dooms itself to be cast aside in man's upward struggle towards the natural goals of freedom, power and love. It will cease to be truly "Christian".'[3]

Thirdly, Appendix B shows that analytic theory and practice has continued to develop beyond Freud. Not only did

Jung break away from Freud, partly because he ascribed a
more positive role to the spiritual and to religion; other
'Freudian' writers have built upon his early work to develop
an even more sophisticated understanding of human personality. Some are positive about religious faith, others are
agnostic. But to dismiss any examination of what psychologists have to say because they lack Christian conviction is
as foolish as dismissing the work of any other scientist
simply on such grounds.

Pastoral counselling cannot, of course, be divorced from
the spiritual and the theological. It is a specialized approach
to counselling which will become clearer in its distinctiveness
if we first delineate some of the boundaries of those whose
work is primarily concerned with the human personality. It is
surprising how many people are unaware of the differences
between those who practise in the psychological field. At the
risk of stating the obvious I will describe briefly the work of
the psychologist, the psychoanalyst and the psychotherapist,
taking the last on to some of the distinctions between therapy
and counselling, and the particular place of pastoral
counselling.

Psychiatrists are not necessarily interested in psychotherapy
or in counselling, and should not be confused with psychoanalysts. Psychiatrists are doctors who have specialized in
the treatment of mental disorders. Some of them see mental
illness as being mainly a dysfunction of the brain or of
chemical imbalance. Those who hold this view favour the use
of psychotropic drugs to change the biochemical balance of
the body, thus affecting particular areas of the brain. They
may advocate, where necessary, neuro-surgery or electro-
convulsive therapy. Other psychiatrists see mental disorder
as more due to developmental factors, and so prefer the
'talking' therapies: behavioural or analytic psychotherapy,
group therapy, or therapeutic communities. Such a basic
division (here sharply defined for convenience) is reflected
amongst general practitioners also. Psychiatrists work with
other staff such as clinical psychologists, occupational
therapists, social workers and psychiatric nurses.

A psychologist is not normally a doctor of medicine.
Following a degree in psychology, he or she may train in a
specialized area, the one concerning us here being clinical

psychology. As such he is responsible for psychological testing (I.Q., personality, aptitude and projective tests) and also for therapy. While the main bias of clinical psychologists tends to be towards behavioural psychotherapy (see Appendix B), they also train as psychotherapists who use analytic techniques. Like some doctors and psychiatrists there are some psychologists who will use counselling methods or counselling skills in their work.

Psychoanalysts are few in number, and are usually either doctors or clinical psychologists as well. The training is a lengthy and expensive one, and the term psychoanalyst (or analytical psychologist in the case of Jungians) is usually reserved for those who are members of their own particular professional society. Psychotherapists can also be members of their own societies or associations, although it is a term which is at present used more loosely, and may therefore signify little more than a person's own nomenclature for his work. Psychoanalysis is a confusing term since it is used in two senses: firstly it refers to a method of treatment consisting strictly speaking of four or five hour-long sessions a week, often going on over a period of years; secondly it refers to a theory of personality structure and formation, and to a broad theory of method. There is also a somewhat briefer method of treatment, based on psychoanalysis, which is often known as analytic or psychodynamic psychotherapy.[4]

Psychoanalysis as a treatment was not always as lengthy as it has become. Ernest Jones records how Freud apparently cured the composer Mahler of impotence during a lengthy walk in the park![5] Since it became both a research method (and also a means of livelihood!) treatment lengthened so that in its full form it is only really available to those who have sufficient time and means. Psychotherapy is more common, being financially more viable, and, because it is limited to one or two sessions weekly, is available to greater numbers of people. But even psychotherapy can be expensive of money and of time if it goes on for more than a few months, so that there have been developments over the last twenty years leading to brief or focal psychotherapy. F. Alexander in Chicago was using such methods in the thirties, although he was criticized at the time for watering down the 'pure gold of analysis'. The work of the Tavistock Clinic in London, and of

D. H. Malan and his colleagues in particular, has however demonstrated the possibilities of effective treatment over a period of about thirty weekly sessions.⁶ Although careful selection of patients is clearly one reason for success, Malan also isolates the use of transference (see chapter 9) working with the ending of the contract (see chapter 6), and focussing on particular issues as being essential for change.

There are many other approaches now available to the helper, and some have little obvious connection with the psychodynamic tradition. In view of the proliferation of methods, it is difficult to avoid generalizations, but it is perhaps possible to say that much that goes by the name of counselling differs from brief psychotherapy in being even shorter, and in not using the transference, at least explicitly. This does not mean that the interaction between counsellor and client is of less significance. Nor does it mean that counselling, because it is normally shorter, need be any the less 'deep'. Length does not always equal depth, as many a psychotherapist could demonstrate from work with highly defended clients. We need to define more carefully what we mean by depth, since some of the more emotive counselling techniques certainly appear to touch depths of feeling. But depth is also a metaphor which describes the various 'layers' of the mind, the conscious, the pre-conscious (memory) and the unconscious. Although it is probable that long-term counselling or therapy enables there to be more refined insight, and may be the necessary treatment where a person has been suffering for many years, even the briefest of counselling can on occasion reach very rapidly and deeply into memory, as well as expose deep feelings.

Psychotherapists sometimes use a term called 'the triangle of insight'. The three points of the triangle are: A — past relationships, feelings and events; B — present relationships feelings and events in the everyday life of the client; and C — the relationship between the therapist and the client, together with reactions evoked via the therapeutic relationship. Transference interpretations, as we shall see later, try to make the link clear between all three points of the triangle; for example, 'You seem to take my remarks as being critical of you, just as you find it difficult to accept compliments from your colleagues at work — it shows how much your punitive upbringing has got inside you, so that you see threats in many of the things said to you.'

Most counselling tends to work with two of the three points of the triangle, and most often with A and B, or B and C. Where consistent use is made of all three, or more use made of A and C, counselling becomes much more like psychotherapy. So, the counsellor may observe, and encourage his client to observe, how he reacts to the counsellor in similar ways as he reacts with others currently, or he may demonstrate ways in which past experience is influencing present experience. It is less common for counsellors to make links between past relationships and the present one with the counsellor himself.

What's in a name? It is undoubtedly true that at times the lines between psychotherapy and psychodynamically-based counselling cannot be too finely drawn. It would be pedantic to make too hard and fast a distinction, although it is not a question purely of academic interest. Active use of transference interpretation can make the relationship between therapist and client deeper and more complex, and it is therefore part of the responsibility of the counsellor to ensure that the use of the transference is only made when there is sufficient evidence both that the client can tolerate it, and that the counsellor himself has the expertise which can work with intense personal feelings towards him. This book is about recognizing one's limitations, as well as opportunities.

What of 'pastoral counselling' or 'pastoral psychotherapy' (a less common expression in Britain)? One possible confusion must be clarified. 'Pastoral' has come to mean care, welfare, and counselling work practised in schools by teachers or school counsellors. Though this is now in common use in educational circles, it is not the sense in which it is used here. Reference to 'pastoral counselling' or 'pastoral care' here is to the work of men and women for whom religious faith is a major concern, for whom theological reflection is important, and who perhaps work in the context of a religious setting.

Counsellors, like other helpers, can specialize in particular areas of concern, or they may work with specific groups of people. Student counsellors, school counsellors or youth counsellors all work predominantly with one age group. Others, such as marriage guidance counsellors, pregnancy

counsellors, or careers counsellors, specialize in working with
areas of fairly narrow concern, but across a wider age span.
The description of the counsellor or the counselling service
provides a way in for clients, who will probably present him
with a problem about marriage, career choice, etc. Yet the
counselling need not confine itself to the problem presented.
Sexual problems, for instance, may exist in isolation, but it is
far more likely that they will be symptomatic of the other
difficulties which beset intimate relationships. The pastoral
counsellor may be approached because he appears to be a
representative of religious concerns, but he will find that the
initial problems are not necessarily confined to religious
matters, and that even those which are require wider
exploration. The pastoral counsellor's connection with
religious belief and practice will make him a person whom
some will approach because they fear that other ways of help
may be critical of, or destructive of, their belief. As such they
have a set of assumptions which the pastoral counsellor
needs to recognize and may need to work through; it may at
times be important for him to question their version of 'the
faith'. Others might equally avoid the pastoral counsellor for
opposite reasons, fearing that 'pastoral' is equivalent to
'preaching', and that religious answers are going to be
imposed upon them. Identification with the church or with a
religious faith can be either a help or a handicap, and the
pastoral counsellor needs to be aware of what his particular
'label' means to those who approach him for help.

One definition of 'pastoral counselling' is that it is an
activity carried out within the context of the religious
community. There is another definition of pastoral counselling
which overlaps this, of counselling which recognizes the
importance of ultimate concerns to human beings, and which
accepts questions about life and death, about existence, values
and meaning as valid questions. Although the pastoral
counsellor will not find that every client asks such questions,
especially when more immediate crises predominate, he will
work with some people who move beyond initial problems to
an exploration of self and others which embraces the deeper
questions about life. Such areas can be as threatening and
bewildering as issues of daily living, consisting as they do of
enigmatic matters which may vex the pastoral counsellor as

much as the client. Since he is involved in this type of work, the pastor is probably not one of those churchmen who finds all the answers clearly stated in the Bible or in dogmatic theology. The theological centrality of 'incarnation', of 'the word made flesh', means that the pastoral counsellor takes humanity seriously, but he also takes seriously the problems which arise from reflection upon the significance of man in the world.

Such a description of pastoral counselling does not imply that other counsellors do not share these concerns, or that their clients do not voice them. However much we like to compartmentalize, specialized areas of counselling unavoidably overlap. There are many counsellors, working in other contexts, who also ask themselves these deeper questions, even though they do not necessarily subscribe to a particular religious faith. Philosophical, political and ethical thinking—whether Christian, Jewish, Buddhist, Humanist or Marxist—contributes to the value system of the counsellor, and informs his view of man and society. If it is necessary to draw distinctions, perhaps the pastoral counsellor can be said to take a particular interest in man's search for understanding, not only of himself and his immediate context, but also of the total context in which he finds himself.

In practice the pastoral counsellor moves between basic human issues, and theological and spiritual exploration. Sometimes they will be inextricably woven together as his studies in psychology and theology complement each other. The following example demonstrates the choices facing the pastoral counsellor as he listened to a young man who came to see him, whether to take up the problems of 'the flesh' or 'the spirit'.

Colin was in his early twenties, and had come to the priest after his doctor had referred him, aware of how much part the young man's faith played in his problems. Colin was obsessed with the meaning of the 'sin against the Holy Spirit' for which Christ said there was no forgiveness. He had searched avidly through the Bible and biblical commentaries to try and find out whether God really punished sinners. His sin, as he felt it, was that he was a homosexual.

The first time they met, the counsellor explored with Colin what he meant by saying he was a homosexual. It soon turned out that he had never had a homosexual relationship, but that what really concerned him was masturbation, which was always accompanied by fantasies that he was being humiliated by another man. Colin described himself as always having been isolated, and when younger he was often bullied. His religious belief had ranged from a brief involvement with Jehovah's Witnesses to a small evangelical group in which he now was. This group was clearly very supportive to him, and they had tried, unsuccessfully, to convince him of God's forgiveness.

To the pastoral counsellor it was obvious that Colin's two problems were linked. His fantasies of humiliation were linked to experiences of humiliation when younger; and furthermore his picture of God was of one who humiliates sinners. Where was the counsellor to start? With Colin's perception of himself, or his picture of God? The latter had not changed despite the efforts of his evangelical friends. The counsellor decided to aim his comments at trying to relieve some of the shame about masturbation, and to lead Colin towards seeing that he found it difficult to accept himself. Since the sexual fantasy pointed to an orientation which seemed fairly fixed, the counsellor felt that for the time being he would leave that problem on one side. So he pointed out to Colin how his image of God portrayed him as vindictive, rather like the boys who bullied him when he was a young teenager; and also how he might himself have felt towards his persecutors. This made it difficult for him to allow himself to believe that he was forgiven.

However, when they met for a second time, Colin said rather more about his fantasies. Sometimes he was able to climax when he thought of himself as a 'pet' being fondled by a sexually experienced woman. The counsellor felt that there was a sign here of some movement in sexual orientation, and he was able to convey to Colin his feeling that he did not always have to see himself as isolated, because of his fear of homosexual relationships. Given help he might be able to move towards relating more fully to women. They both agreed to look at these problems—the sexual, and the doubts which he had about God's forgiveness.

This brief example shows how the spiritual and the psychological aspects mingle, with one influencing the other. It also shows how the pastoral counsellor tried to focus on one issue, but was ready to broaden that focus when he perceived a hopeful sign of movement in the further description of the fantasies. It is also possible to see how the earlier distinction made between pastoral psychotherapy and pastoral counselling holds true. If in the relationship with the counsellor Colin had shown either fear of being humiliated, or even a wish to be humiliated, the pastor could point this out to Colin, thus completing the third side of the triangle of insight—being bullied when young, being humiliated in fantasy now, seeing God as another humiliator, and perceiving the counsellor as one who would also humiliate him.

There is one further distinction to be made, already alluded to in chapter 1, between pastoral counselling and pastoral care. Again there is an overlap, since counselling is used in this book to describe both a specific task—what we might call formal counselling, within certain boundaries of time, frequency of meeting, and most probably in the counsellor's office—and a general approach to listening and responding to people. The latter could be called informal counselling. The ministry of pastoral care provides many opportunities for this informal approach, using counselling skills and knowledge of human development. The boundaries are frequently less definite, but this need not prevent people talking and expressing themselves more fully. Knowledge of personality development, normal and abnormal, which is essential in formal counselling, is no less valuable in pastoral care. Recognition of the way in which people use defences against seeing themselves as they are, the way in which the helper can be regarded as a transference figure, and other topics which are covered in later chapters, can enhance the work of pastoral care as much as more formal counselling. Pastoral care contains other aspects than counselling alone, but within the context of a visit to a home, the preparation of a couple for marriage, in the few words which can be exchanged with mourners when on crematorium duty, or in the casual encounter in the street, the conversation can provide opportunities to go deeper than pleasantries or clichéd phrases.

Although this is possible, it is not simply done. The pastor who meets a person for a greater length of time, in the quietness of his own room, and in a situation where a person has asked for help, can engage more easily in that activity which we call counselling. It is not easy even then to step back and see what is happening. It is even more difficult to do this in an informal interaction, which provides less time to reflect, and where distractions from other people are more likely to make concentration difficult. It is sometimes less easy for those who know or are known to the pastor, and who meet him in other settings, to be frank and open about their emotions.

Pastors can be involved in pastoral counselling as well as in pastoral care. Each aspect of the work will enhance the other. Pastoral care will involve meeting people in their homes, and understanding issues in person which are talked about in counselling. Similarly the practice of more formal counselling enables the skills acquired to be more naturally applied in pastoral care. While pastors (and other helpers) will not wish to become full-time counsellors, there will always be opportunities for seeing some people in a more defined counselling contract, and to apply that experience and learning to the total ministry.

As Bernard Mobbs observes[7] the role of the counsellor does not always lie easily alongside the role of the parish priest. This is probably a more difficult situation than it is for the social worker or for the psychiatrist who chooses to see some people for more formal counselling. Like the general practitioner (for whom it can be difficult to combine the necessary physical examination of patients with formally counselling them) the clergyman meets his own parishioners in other settings and in other roles, as preacher, teacher, chairman of committees and friend. This puts limitations on formal counselling which will need to be borne in mind in later chapters. Given team ministries, or co-operation between clergy and lay pastors in other parishes, there can be referral from one area to another. Not all the pastor's contacts, hopefully, are with people who attend his (or any) church.

Where the person does not know the pastoral counsellor in other roles, the more formal parts of what follows can still be applicable.

Notes

1. See Appendix C: Further Reading; also chapter 10.
2. See, e.g., H. L. Philp, *Freud and Religious Belief.* Rockcliff, London, 1956.
3. R. S. Lee, *Freud and Christianity.* Penguin 1967, p. 176.
4. 'Psychodynamic' describes an approach to and understanding of mental and emotional problems, which concentrates on the internal workings of the mind and the relationship between 'parts' of the 'self' (particularly their conflict and their balance), as opposed to a more stable view of states of mind. These internal relationships influence external relations.
5. Ernest Jones, *The Life and Work of Sigmund Freud.* Penguin 1964, pp. 358-9.
6. See D. H. Malan, *The Frontier of Brief Psychotherapy.* Plenum Medical Books 1976, and other books by the same author.
7. In an unpublished essay on pastoral care and counselling.

PART TWO

Techniques and Practice of Pastoral Counselling

THREE

First Steps

There are certain features common to most counselling
approaches. The pastoral counsellor primarily seeks to create
an atmosphere in which the person who has come to him, or
whom he has called to see, can express himself freely—what
he thinks and what he feels. In one sense we could describe
the counselling manner as that of the good conversationalist.
The difference, however, between counselling and most social
situations is that the counsellor tries to say as little as
possible, while at the same time encouraging the other to say
as much as he can. This requires training, because definite
skills need to be learned.

Furthermore some of those who ask for help are in fact
reluctant to express themselves fully, for one reason or
another. This requires even greater skill on the part of the
counsellor. For the time being I will concentrate upon the
primary techniques which the counsellor can use to facilitate
the flow of expression in the person who is well-motivated,
and sufficiently self-aware to be able to benefit from a
situation where he can monitor for himself what he says
aloud—given, that is, a counsellor who encourages him to do
this.

It may seem artificial to use 'techniques'. Pastoral training
in the past has assumed that clergy possess the right personal
qualities by virtue of their calling, just as medical training
still tends to assume that the 'bedside manner' or 'tender
loving care' are part of the academic brilliance required for
entry into medical school. 'Techniques' are not the same as
'tricks', and nothing sinister is intended, although clearly
such techniques can be misused.

The analogy that comes to mind is of learning to drive. In
this chapter I describe fundamental skills which in themselves
serve to increase the pastor's capacity to listen and gently

explore what is said. When listening to people who can verbalize their thoughts and feelings (which does not require people who are well-educated, as some critics suggest) it is often sufficient to use simply these basic skills, just as when learning to drive it would not take long to master steering, changing gear and braking as long as one were driving on a deserted racing circuit.

Unfortunately, if you wish to pass a driving test you are not permitted to take it in ideal conditions. The real difficulties for the learner driver come from the inescapable presence of other road-users, and from having to use the car on roads which have sharp corners, steep hills, traffic lights and pedestrian crossings. In order to use a car you also have to learn how to reverse round corners, make three-point turns, park in small places, and execute other necessary manoeuvres. So too in counselling there are complications. Not every person is from the beginning highly perceptive, verbal, or well-motivated. So although every counselling approach worthy of the name emphasizes the value of listening, remembering, understanding, and relating, this will not be enough in some situations. While some will be helped beyond measure by being able to talk openly to a person who listens carefully to them, and who accepts them without harsh criticism, other people will present the pastoral counsellor with equivalent difficulties to the learner who takes the car on to the busy high street. For instance, even the person who appears to be talking freely may in fact be preventing the helper from making his own contribution. Some of the difficulties which are encountered will cause little worry, and will be dealt with naturally. Others are less easy, and even less obvious. These require constant refinement of basic skills and understanding, and some of these refinements will be examined in later chapters.

In order to help the flow of the conversation, the pastoral counsellor needs to keep to certain 'rules'. These rules are not hard and fast laws, which can never be broken. Frequently they are framed as 'avoid . . .', with the proviso that always should be added '. . . where possible'. In training courses those who learn these first steps initially find it difficult to follow such guidelines without becoming over self-conscious. I see no easy way out of this—again it is like those first few driving lessons, when it takes time for the manoeuvres learned to become second-nature, an extension of oneself, as natural as walking or breathing.

The 'rules' which are basic to counselling are:

1. *Listen*, and listen with undivided attention. I shall qualify this as we go on, but for the moment try to absorb this point. We rarely listen to people so carefully that we put out of mind our own concerns, our own constructions on what they are saying, or even our own prejudices. We often hear what we want to hear, not what is being said; we remember some details and we forget others. We take as important what we find interesting, and not necessarily what the other regards as most significant. Exercises 1 and 2 in Appendix A demonstrate some of the problems of listening, and give some experience in listening without having to add our own words or interpretations.

2. *Remember.* Remembering is easier when we listen carefully, and when we keep what we say to a minimum. Remembering is important, not just because the events, details, the significant little phrases and words will help us to understand what a client has experienced; it is also a way of demonstrating our care, and our attentiveness. When a person remembers our name, having met us briefly in the past, we feel important and valued. When the helper can remember the names, the dates, or what a person has said from week to week, this too conveys openly that positive regard for the importance of the other, which counselling trainers describe as central to effective helping.

   Pastors and other helpers are busy people, and they meet many in the course of their work. It is not always possible to remember details in such circumstances. Careful listening at the time, however, enables the helper to make notes after the person has left. It is unwise to make notes when listening, because this too readily creates a clinical atmosphere, and also prevents the helper from observing facial and other non-verbal expressions. There are different ways of recording (tape-recorders, verbatim accounts, summaries of sessions) which each helper will have his own view upon. Those wishing to follow up some of these methods of recording in more detail are referred to two articles in the journal *Counselling*.[1]

3. *Relax*, and do all that is possible to help the person talking to you to relax. Not every counselling opportunity comes in your own room or office, but if it does try to ensure that your room conveys a sense of calm and peace — without jarring pictures or *objets d'art*; by ensuring privacy and freedom from interruption (especially where possible the telephone), and by providing seating which is comfortable. It scarcely needs pointing out that 'interviews' conducted on straight chairs, or with the helper behind a desk are not conducive to the quiet stillness which underlies the counselling approach. Place chairs at an angle, so that there is no 'eyeball-to-eyeball' confrontation, but so that each person can still observe and look at the other. Above all, and this is difficult when there is so much else to occupy the mind, try in your own person and mannerisms to convey a calm and accepting attitude. This extends to facial expression, stillness of the body, and avoiding non-verbally some of the responses which I shall shortly describe as being counter-productive.

4. *Listen beneath the obvious.* Having encouraged you to relax, I now make matters rather more complicated! While listening to the details, and remembering the words and expressions, try also to listen at another level, to the less obvious feelings and thoughts which may be around. Exercise 3 in Appendix A may help begin this type of awareness. People often speak of themselves or of others in one way, while conveying in their tone of voice or gestures different, sometimes diametrically opposed, feelings. This aspect of listening is like trying to spot the bass line of a piece of music, while still concentrating upon the melody on the top line. Try to draw out these underlying feelings and thoughts where they are not as apparent to the person speaking as they are to you, although you may have to do this tentatively to test out whether your own perception is in fact correct.

5. *Listen also to yourself*, and to the still, small voice within. Here is yet another dimension to listening, sometimes

called the 'third ear'. Imagine yourself in the speaker's situation, and how you might have reacted had it been you. Be careful, because your reaction might not have been the same, and might have been inappropriate, but if there are some grounds for thinking that you are in tune with what this person was experiencing, you can suggest what you have in mind. But put it in the terms of the other person, and not yourself. Avoid relating your own experiences and feelings directly: e.g. it is not helpful to say, 'I was in that situation once, it was dreadful . . . I would have done this . . . or felt that . . .' The pastor is not there to tell his own life-story; nor should he presume that his response would have been the right one; neither does he try to elicit sympathy for himself. Use your own experience where possible to suggest, again tentatively, other dimensions to the situation being described: e.g. 'I wonder whether you felt . . . Is it possible that you are now feeling . . .' This and the above point embrace what many counselling manuals call 'empathy'—the ability to put yourself in the shoes of the person speaking, and from that position to reflect some of the feelings and thoughts, obvious or hidden, which he might be experiencing. Exercise 4 in Appendix A gives some practice in this and the remaining points.

6. *Avoid speaking too soon*, too often and too much. You are trying to help a person to tell his own story, and to develop it. There are different ways of facilitating this, such as summing up periodically what has been said, but in a few words:

> 'I don't go out much. I'm getting on now, and I find the hill too much for me. I haven't got any family living nearby anymore, and my wife died last year. The trouble is I was made redundant five years ago, and don't see my mates at work anymore. I've got all sorts of problems.'
> 'Life sounds very lonely.'

The response sounds obvious, but such a response often is enough to help a person expand upon the feelings of

loneliness. Alternatively, pick up the last phrase, reflect it
back, or re-phrase it. This too can lead a person to develop
what they are saying. Imagine the person saying what has
been described above, but with this alternative response:
'All sorts of problems?'

7. *Keep questions to a minimum* (except the rhetorical
   questions such as those in the response above). Only
   question when you are not clear what is meant, or where
   there is an obscure remark which could lead to more
   definite information which could help you understand.
   Try to make the questions as open-ended as possible.
   Avoid, wherever possible, 'why?' questions, which can be
   very difficult to answer. It is often the case that if a person
   knew the answer 'why?' he would not be seeking help at
   all. Helpers, especially early on in counselling training,
   find questions very tempting; but frequently the questions
   they ask are irrelevant, or are questions which change the
   subject. It is as if questions are used because the helper
   feels he has to say something. There will always be some
   tension between wanting to find out more of a person's
   background and circumstances (especially when long-term
   counselling necessitates building up a form of case-history)
   and listening to what a person wishes to say now. Reserve
   relevant questions which are not immediately connected
   with what is being described for those moments when you
   both seem really stuck for words.
       For example, if we take the words above as a starting
   point for the counsellor's response, it would be inappropriate to ask, 'Why do you say you've got problems?' It
   would be possible to ask, 'What problems do you have?',
   or 'When did you begin to feel the problems getting on top
   of you?' or 'How do you feel?', although in that particular
   example even some of these questions can be avoided in
   favour of the more open responses already indicated in (6).

8. *Avoid making loaded remarks or judgements.* Such responses are what people most fear (or even expect) from
   authority figures such as clergy and doctors. Phrases such
   as 'Why on earth did you do that?' or 'That was a foolish
   thing to do', or even apparently more gentle phrases like
   'That was unwise', may drive a person away at worst, or

prevent them from being open at best. Where possible, and where necessary, try to help a person make their own assessment of themselves or of their actions, e.g. 'Did that work?', 'How did you feel that went down?', 'What else might you have done (said) in those circumstances?'. Exercise 5 in Appendix A examines appropriate and inappropriate responses to some of the 'revelations' of those who come for help.[2] The various types of loaded remark which should be avoided include exclamations of surprise or shock (facially as well as verbally), expressions of over-concern, ridicule, blame, rejection, intolerance, flattery or undue praise, and unnecessary reassurance. At the same time as avoiding such expression, the counsellor should extend reassurance when it is really necessary, express open-mindedness, even towards irrational attitudes, respect the right of the others to hold different values and preferences, and should be able to express sympathy when it seems important.

These then are the main ground-rules when engaging in counselling. Some will seem like common-sense, and only natural after all — this is true, although we do not always act in common-sense or natural ways. All are elementary, in the sense of being basic skills, not in the sense of being simple. And although I now move on to look at some of the complications which arise in counselling, both for the counsellor and the person whom he listens to, such rapid exposition does little justice to the time which it will take to allow these elementary skills to become second nature.

Notes

1. *Counselling* No. 36, April 1981, obtainable from the British Association for Counselling, 37a Sheep Street, Rugby, CV21 3BX. The articles referred to are my own 'Setting the Record Straight' and Dr Dryden's 'Some Uses of Audio-Tape Procedures in Counselling: A Personal View'.

2. A useful summary of many of these 'sundry rules' upon which Exercise 5 is based, will be found in L. R. Wolberg's *The Technique of Psychotherapy*. Heinemann 1967, pp. 584-90

FOUR

Starting with Oneself

It may not be immediately obvious that the person who wishes to counsel has to start by understanding himself. Helping is often seen as putting others first, at some personal cost. Although personal satisfaction is clearly part of the helping relationship, it is not always given enough recognition, since there are needs in the helper which we need to acknowledge if the counselling relationship is to be effective. In this chapter I wish to look at some of the less obvious characteristics of the helping person which can, if unrecognized, get in the way, and cause discomfort to pastor and client. At worst these hidden factors might lead to emotional damage to either person.

These are strong words, and necessarily so. Counselling is always open to the criticism that it represents interference and intrusion into another person's life. There are people who mean well, but who cause more suffering than they cure. The counsellor takes his task seriously when he is requested to share the intimate thoughts and feelings of another. His responsibility is as great as that of any other person whose service affects human life, whether it be the surgeon or the car mechanic. There are life-and-death issues at stake. I do not mean by this the risk of suicide — which is commonly the fear which people have when helping others, lest they make mistakes which lead to self-damage by the client. Although we should not underestimate such risks, they are less common than other risks. Since counselling frequently involves helping people with important life decisions, emotional health or emotional damage are alternative outcomes of the helping process.

This responsibility is all the greater because the basic tool of the pastoral counsellor is himself, a self which includes his own wishes and fears. Like the teacher, his effectiveness depends to some extent upon his personality. But to take the example of the surgeon, the rapport between himself and his patient before an operation may help, even if it is not essential. The car mechanic needs technical skills, but these do not depend overmuch upon his moods, unless one day he is so distracted by personal pressures that he is slapdash in his work. In different jobs the relationship between technical skills and the use of one's own personality varies. Counsellors need the skills described in this book, but skills alone are not sufficient. They also need to be aware of the conscious and hidden factors in themselves which influence others. It is therefore essential that we prepare ourselves for this work by beginning a continuous self-examination which underpins all the technical learning. Since the pastor sees self-knowledge as one of the aims of his counselling the client, he cannot expect less of himself. 'Physician, heal thyself.' As Hugh Eadie writes in one of a series of articles on the health of the clergy: 'Considering his potential influence on the lives of those to whom he ministers, the clergyman's health has pragmatic, psychological and theological repercussions which cannot be treated casually.'[1]

I can only deal with this area generally here, although I will inevitably touch upon personal factors in many of my readers. What follows may (hopefully) mean that some discover aspects of themselves of which they had previously been unaware. This may be painful, or may cause anxiety. It is difficult to read books on psychology without discovering aspects of oneself therein. Some become very concerned at such points. Since it is my intention to encourage self-analysis and self-understanding, but not to make people uncomfortable, some caveats are necessary before proceeding further.

First, some of the ideas I consider are based upon research, but there will always be arguments about the amount of weight which can be attached to opinions and statistics, especially in such a delicate area. Since it is claimed (by Hugh Eadie, for instance) that up to two-thirds of clergy (and by implication other helpers) show some of the characteristics I shall examine, we need to be careful how we use such evidence. Statistics produce generalizations from the particular. Not every motivation or personal characteristic applies to every helper. What follows can only be a guide to thinking.

Since most of us are adept at deluding ourselves when faced with ideas too near the truth, the reader who fails to recognize himself in any of the descriptions might need to take a closer look. Yet helpers can be over-critical of themselves, as Eadie himself points out, so we should also be wary of looking for trouble!

Secondly, these general points may provide an incentive for further reflection, but book knowledge is no substitute for self-knowledge. In each helper we can expect there to be variations on a common theme. Such self-understanding is best gained through interaction with others. A responsible pastoral counselling ministry should include regular super-vision, either individually or in a group, either with peers or with a more experienced tutor. Other people are often able to observe, because they are at one remove, features of counselling practice which are not obvious to the person who is close to the action. Another aspect of training which every counsellor should seriously consider is to experience for himself, as client, the counselling process. It seems to be a characteristic of many helpers that they find it difficult to admit they themselves need help. Some may find it more palatable by calling it 'training'.

Thirdly, amongst the 'sundry rules' of basic counselling set out in the previous chapter, was acceptance of the other and whatever he says, without horror, without damaging criticism, and without rejection. To accept is not to condone, but it is essential to accept before going on to examine particular behaviour, thoughts and feelings. Those who work in the helping professions, particularly when in training, do not find it easy to admit what appear to them to be 'faults', especially when self-assessment is closely bound up with assessment for professional qualification. The examination of ourselves which follows is not intended as an exercise in cleansing the temple, or sorting the sheep from the goats. Only by accepting what we find within, even if occasionally it seems shocking, can we go deeper than superficial shame or guilt towards a level of insight which not only bears upon counselling practice, but which also leads to greater fulfilment for the helper.

In essence then, the characteristics of the helping person are 'neutral'—each feature in the helper can be used constructively as well as destructively. Where there have been fears about aspects of oneself, the recognition and acceptance of them can release the helper to work more effectively. Where wishes are discovered which are over-strong, understanding of them may help temper their influence, and so minimize the risks of manipulating the client.

A social worker was afraid to confront her clients with their manipulative behaviour. They were often out when she called. She found herself being persuaded to take their side against other agencies, and she felt that she generally went along too readily with what her clients expected of her. She complained to her supervisor that she found it difficult to show her anger, yet she came away from some of her interviews full of resentment.

It is not uncommon for helpers to have problems with the handling of anger. If she were able to feel more at ease with her angry feelings, she could confront her clients more easily. But that is not to say that there was no value in her being 'slow to anger', because others might have vented such feelings impulsively and destructively, which of course is what she feared doing. The supervisor helped her to get in touch with her anxieties about her anger, so that she was then able to confront, but in a way which was thought out. At one and the same time she could then preserve the trust which she felt to be so important, but was also able to demonstrate that she was not soft. Accepting the fact that she could get very angry helped her to recognize when she needed to confront; but by using her natural disposition towards a gentle approach, she was able to express herself sufficiently forcefully to make her point, but not so bluntly as to destroy the confidence her clients had in her.

Eric Rayner observes in his book on *Human Development* that work entails mastery of skills, and also of anxieties. The dustman has to master disgust, the pilot the fear of heights, or a nurse the fear of death.[2] The particular anxieties which many counsellors have are about handling feelings of love, aggression, sexuality and power. Training for pastoral counselling requires some mastery of the anxiety about such feelings, whether they are shown by clients, or are seen in different forms in counsellors themselves.

One of the most obvious motivations of the pastor and other helpers is the need to be seen as useful, compassionate and loving towards others. Such an ideal contributes to the patience and tolerance of the pastoral counsellor. But as soon as we set up such an ideal, there is danger of it becoming over-idealized, and of creating an 'anti-ideal' which must at all times be avoided. As helpers, therefore, we tend to feel we should not be concerned for ourselves, and that we must not get impatient, angry or dependent upon others. Love must be pure, non-possessive and asexual. Areas are created which contain taboo feelings, which are then repressed. Such repression of negative or selfish feelings (as they are thought to be) can impose considerable stress on the helper. He may absorb such feelings until he can contain them no longer; then they burst out, or he turns against himself. He may find himself employing more subtle ways of expressing such forbidden feelings. For example, anger bottled up may turn into resentment of all those who want help, or can be turned back on the self, so that the helper experiences less and less self-esteem. He may convert the anger into missing appointments, changing times round, starting late, putting some of his interventions across in rather vindictive ways, or even taking out his frustrations on others outside the job — spouses and families can easily become the recipients of exaggerated and unjustified reactions brought home from work with clients. Helpers seem to find it more difficult to tolerate such negative feelings in themselves, when they readily accept them in those they help. All counsellors should look again at the second Gospel commandment: Love your neighbour, as *yourself.*

Those who devote their lives to loving and caring for others often need to be loved and cared for themselves, but feel that they have to push down that need. This does not prevent such needs coming out in other ways, looking for admiration and approval. They often receive praise, at least to their faces, for the sacrifices they make and the valuable work they do. Behind their backs is another matter, for some will actually call them 'mugs' or 'gluttons for punishment'. It is natural to want to be useful, but in counselling it is difficult to measure usefulness. Results can be a long time coming. Again it is normal to want one's work to be valued, but too much need for external affirmation from clients can lead to difficulties in allowing them to express their frustration with the counsellor who cannot be the 'saviour' they wished for. Helpers may find it difficult to accept criticism or anger expressed towards them by their clients. But the wish of the helper to maintain his self-respect may result in opportunities for others to express themselves more fully being lost.

One way of caring for oneself, especially when early upbringing has stressed the importance of being 'unselfish' is to project the unloved part of oneself on to the client, and surround him with the care and attention one wishes for. The danger then arises both of neglecting one's own needs, and neglecting the client's negative feelings. The pastor who has a simplistic, over-optimistic view of human nature may not spot those people who will take advantage of him, and who constantly test out his patience. Some people do not seem to change, however much love is showered upon them. They destroy loving gestures, they ignore the positive affirmation made by the helper: they soak up love and concern, but it makes little difference. Some of the most angry of people are also the nicest of people, who express anger passively. They succeed in making the helper feel frustrated and angry. Many people are helped at the point when they can recognize their own negative feelings, and can express them in a safe situation. So the helper who gives and gives, who fails to notice such passive-aggressive behaviour, and who denies his own anger and frustration, may unwittingly be doing a disservice. It is like giving money to the alcoholic down-and-out, who then abuses the helper's generosity by spending it on more drink, and so is prevented from facing up to the desperation of his condition.

The counsellor who needs admiration is prone to hang on to those people who tell him how valuable he is, and who flatter him in other ways. He may favour people who are attractive, in personality or in physical appearance, or those who are 'good' clients, saying all the right things, unaware that some of these people are anxious to convey a good impression because they fear being rejected if they show their less flattering side. If he is desperate to be useful, the helper may give too long a time, or too frequent appointments to those in distress, or may drop everything to respond to a cry

of distress, without first assessing the seriousness of the
situation. Responding blindly to others' needs is not just bad
practice. Some people, who are particularly hungry for love,
also feel guilty about having their demands met, and may
break off from the counsellor who responds too readily. They
are frightened of the power they have over others. If such
people do not break off contact, the counsellor may begin to
feel drained and increasingly tired, and may even consider
breaking off the help he himself gives by referring them
elsewhere. (This may, of course, be necessary when a person's
condition is too much for the skills of a pastoral counsellor.
What is being described here however is passing a person on
out of sheer desperation, and not as a result of careful thought
and planning.)

All this may seem an ominous picture, although it is one
which helpers will find rings true of some of their more
difficult clients. When the pastoral counsellor depends upon
his clients to affirm his ideal self-image, there will always be
some people who will play along with his wishes, while there
will be others who seem to go out of their way to destroy that
good image. Justification by works has been appropriately
criticized at various points in the history of the church.
Helpers need to try to love themselves for themselves, and
not to rely upon work alone to prove themselves. There are
other places in the helper's life (at home, for instance) where
it is more appropriate to look for love.

This is not to deny that it also matters to do a job well, and
to take pride in one's abilities as a pastor. But pastoral
counselling means much more than loving and caring. It may
include being able to accept compliments, but also being able
to take the criticism, some of it unjustified, with equanimity.
The counsellor has to be open to receive a wider range of
responses, not just positive ones. He also needs to learn to see
both praise and criticism as not necessarily being a statement
about himself, but indicative of the way in which the client
responds to others generally.

High ideals are often accompanied by severe self-criticism
and self-denigration when those ideals are not met. Those
whose idealism and energetic work contributes to the good of
others frequently have a more private side of themselves
which feels depressed by failure. The higher the ideals, the

greater the gap there is between what is desired and what is possible, with a consequent feeling of guilt when the gap is not bridged. Clergy may develop a condition which Eadie quotes as 'the hardening of the oughteries'. (Of course it is not only pastors who show some of these attitudes.) The clergyman caught in this particularly vicious spiral may therefore work harder and more frantically to lessen the gap and alleviate the guilt. Such hard work imposes its own stresses, impairs effectiveness, leads to even greater frustration, and so widens even more the gap between the critical and the idealistic parts of the helper's personality. Pastors readily become over-conscientious, but neglect to recognize that in their busy-ness they are as much concerned for their own needs (which are crying out to be recognized and met) as they are for the needs of those whom they help.

In counselling such ambition and zeal takes different forms. The counsellor can be driven to concentrate upon presenting problems and not take time to look at the whole person. Short-term counselling, and indeed some long-term work, benefits from focussing on particular issues, while still allowing the person to decide what he wishes to discuss. But such a focus is not always on initial presenting problems, since these are often only pointers to more central issues.

The pastor who needs to prove his worth by results may find himself trying to solve the client's problem for him, not allowing him to take initiative himself. Provision of material help, the giving of advice, answering questions which the person might well be able to answer himself—all such ways of helping have been mentioned in chapter 1, but they are not 'counselling'. Ultimately there is greater satisfaction for the pastoral counsellor when he sees the other able to find his own solution. It is like the satisfaction of the parent whose child becomes able to do things for himself.

Such active help is not always wrong in counselling, but decisions to give advice or manage a person's life are steps which should be taken only after due consideration of the necessity and the effect of such action. What I draw attention to here is the unthinking response, which arises out of concern for one's image as a helper, rather than out of genuine concern for the welfare of the client.

One way of trying to achieve more obvious results is to

change counselling techniques before considering first why the present approach may not be working. Certain Gestalt techniques, for instance, enable held-back emotions to be expressed more readily—such as hammering a cushion to release pent-up anger. We shall see when we look at defences that there are frequently good reasons for holding back feelings, and that such reasons are as much part of the exploration involved in counselling as the feelings themselves. If the pastoral counsellor's counselling training leads him to feel that catharsis alone is valuable, such techniques may be valid. If however an analytic model forms the framework for counselling, it is not as straightforward as that. Punching a cushion is not the same as punching someone you love. It is the task of counselling, as I see it, to help a person discover less acceptable thoughts and feelings, to understand the reasons for holding them back, and to learn to find appropriate ways of expressing them in the context of close relationships, but in ways which are not disastrous.

Freud once wrote to a friend, 'I would advise you to set aside your therapeutic ambition and try and understand what is happening. When you have done that, therapeutics will take care of itself.'[3] He even mentioned the motto of an early surgeon, commending it to analysts. 'I dressed his wounds, God cured him.'[4] Carl Rogers would express it differently, but with much the same intention, that it is the provision of a climate of trust which enables people to discover the capacity to solve their own problems. When a person is well motivated, counselling helps him to change himself, although the counselling will be only one of the circumstances which enables this to happen. Where motivation to change is less strong, or where there are conflicts which make change more difficult, the pastoral counsellor will be more effective when he can help a person examine his doubts and hesitations. Short-term measures, although they sometimes have temporary effect, are more often than not placebos.

I have devoted some space to two features of the helper—the need to be loving and to be loved, and the idealized self-image which finds criticism or self-criticism hard to accept—because they make it more difficult for the pastor to accept other feelings within himself, since they are felt to be both negative and unloving. These feelings include anger, sexual desires, and the wish to be powerful — perhaps a classical triad of the basic emotions. Let us take a closer look at these feelings, reminding ourselves that since they are often accepted when expressed by others, there is no reason to feel too anxious or guilty at discovering them within oneself.

Those who seek to help others have sometimes suffered themselves, and so wish to help alleviate the sufferings of others. They may also wish to make some reparation for harm which they consciously or unconsciously feel they have caused. One of the difficulties for the counsellor is that his way of helping means having to endure the suffering of others, but at the same time having to suffer helplessness at being unable to alleviate pain. Furthermore, he will at times have to take up the issues which lead in the short-term to pain and anguish. Before the advent of anaesthetics, surgeons must have felt something of the same dilemma, knowing that in order to bring about healing, they had to inflict severe pain. Counselling has no anaesthetics other than the quiet compassion of the counsellor. Unfortunately concern alone does not take away pain, even though it may lessen it.

The pastoral counsellor is human like anyone else — he has compassion, but he also has sadistic wishes. Those occasions when he has to stand by feeling helpless, or when he has to bring pain into the open, will often make him feel uncomfortable, in case he is simply being sadistic. His work is more often than not with people who experience varying degrees of emotional distress, and yet he finds a curious satisfaction in working in such a painful situation. Unless he has come to terms with his own aggression, he may find it difficult to do simple things like disagree, or, more difficult, to express his anger appropriately, or to confront people with sensitive and painful aspects of themselves which they would prefer to avoid.

When such steps are too closely associated to sadistic wishes, counsellors will tend to hold back when they should speak. Too concerned with maintaining a loving ideal, the pastor may find himself on the masochistic end of a sado-masochistic partnership, not daring to contradict or set boundaries, with clients who can become quite punitive towards their helper. Other pastors, unaware of the strength of their anger, may bombard the client and set up a similar partnership, although in this instance it is the client who comes back time and again for punishment.

The pastor may also feel uncomfortable about having sexual feelings. Eadie observes how curious it is that those who are motivated by the 'appeal of loving', and who find it appropriate to be affectionate, gentle and concerned, find it unacceptable to admit sexual, erotic and carnal wishes. He cites some evidence which suggests that clergy and caring professionals generally may be more inhibited and less sexually active than those in other professional groups.[5]

The pastor may therefore feel embarrassed by sexual thoughts about his client, or when sexual feelings are talked about. Sex is much more openly talked about than it has been in the recent past, and some people are more at ease with the admission of sexual problems than they are with problems about hatred, jealousy or aggression. Too keen an interest in sexual matters on the part of the counsellor might lead to intrusive probing into the intimate details of the sexual life of the client, providing him with a vicarious and voyeuristic pleasure, and encouraging inappropriate excitement in the client—a type of mental rape. The helper may be seduced into thinking that sexuality is the only problem, neglecting the many other emotions which abound in interpersonal relationships. On the other hand, too inhibited an attitude towards sexuality can lead to the counsellor avoiding, or refusing to draw out, the sexual problems which the client is hesitant to share.

There is another aspect of loving (which may or may not include the sexual) which is related to this theme. Counselling can be a way of seeking intimacy with another person, while at the same time avoiding it. Eadie draws attention to this feature in some helpers, who engage in a wide range of caring relationships which are distant and safe, but who avoid genuine intimacy. He writes of the clergyman: 'the pulpit, study and vocational image in particular make him a man "set apart", though he overcomes his basic sense of isolation by numerous pastoral relationships'.[6] Helpers may indulge in rich fantasies containing some of their more attractive clients, and engage (without always realizing it) in subtle ways of enjoying sessions together. In some instances this may even extend to a professional relationship which sadly becomes physical and sexual.

The relationship between a counsellor and a client is a curious one, which pastors need to recognize, especially since some clients are themselves not slow to point it out. Harry Guntrip describes the therapist/patient relationship as 'midway between the parent/child relation and the husband/wife relation. It is not a relation between an actual parent, and an actual child, nor is it a relation between two adults on terms of equality. It is a relation between the unhappy and undermined child in the adult patient and a therapist whose own "internal child" ought to have been taken care of by his own training analysis . . .'[7] Guntrip does not go on to qualify what he means by the husband/wife relationship in this analogy. It is clear from what he says about the parent/child relationship that the term 'husband/wife' needs to be treated with caution, since the counselling relationship can only be described as such if viewed in a superficial way.

An anecdote illustrates the difference. It was probably one common grievance which partners in a marriage have which prompted a counsellor's wife to say to him, 'I wish you'd give me some of the time you spend with your clients.' His reply pointed out the fallacy when he said, 'All right. You have an hour a week. What would you like to say?'

Both partners in counselling will probably invest much in their work together, and each in his own way will be temporarily totally involved. It is not, however, the total give and take which is typical of close family ties and friendships. The pastor who looks to those he helps to achieve an intimacy which he cannot achieve elsewhere not only teases them, but deludes himself. Likewise the pastor who avoids the intimacy which legitimately exists in the partnership with the client will need to ask himself if he avoids intimacy generally.

Intimacy there is, but the relationship is not a balanced one. The client is helped and encouraged to share the intimate details of his life, which may give the pastoral counsellor the mistaken impression that he has intimate knowledge of his client. (And the client too can foster this delusion.) There will hopefully be a close rapport between them, but the counsellor chooses, as part of his role, to keep himself in the background, not sharing the details of his own life with the other person. Feelings which a client has for the pastor can sometimes be very strong, and as intense as might be experienced in a marriage. The pastor too may have a wide variety of feelings towards his client at different times, but his training and self-knowledge will help him to subordinate these to the task of helping the client through what Rogers calls 'non-possessive love'. If his own feelings are too intense, the counsellor will need to look within himself in order to reflect upon his counter-transference reactions (see chapter 9).

It is apparent how important the personal needs of the helper are, and how such needs, where too strong or too inhibited, can adversely affect the counselling relationship. It is no exaggeration to suggest that the counsellor is in a position of considerable power, over and above the authority which is often accorded to clergy and other professional people. There is no clear evidence of general attitudes to authority in the helping professions. Evidence is inconsistent as to whether helpers are more prone to being authoritarian or submissive, although I have already suggested that helpers can suffer from quite authoritarian consciences. While some pastors can be too dominant, there are others who are submissive and passive, and allow themselves to be pushed around. The latter in particular are prey for those distressed and apparently passive people who mobilize so much concern and panic around them that they soon discover how powerful their distress can make them over others.

Others hand over all their strength to the helper, making him into the only person who can help them. Such people endow their counsellor with qualities of knowledge and wisdom, and the ability to perform miracles, hanging upon every word that he utters. This can be gratifying to the person who needs to be needed and has to feel important, but pastors will soon become aware of the way in which their words and actions are taken out of context and misunderstood. This is why the counsellor weighs carefully what he wishes to say, so as to be clear and accurate, and as free as possible from distortion.

Some people come to the pastor knowing a little about counselling, but mistakenly believing that non-directiveness means that the counsellor really knows the answers, but is not prepared to give them. They realize that they have to discover their own answers, but imagine that these answers are already in the counsellor's mind waiting to be revealed. In fact the counsellor can only have at best general ideas, especially at the beginning. He has to wait upon the other in order to sharpen his understanding of each person.

A highly intelligent and generally perceptive professional man has been seeing a counsellor for some weeks. On one occasion the counsellor suggested an idea which was on her mind, but about which she was not particularly sure. She wished to check out her own thinking. 'I'm not sure,' she said, 'and I haven't got a complete picture yet, but in my own mind I felt . . .' To her surprise the next meeting started with the man saying to her, 'I must tell you how relieved I was last week when you talked about . . . It wasn't just what you said, but the way you said it. I know rationally that you don't know everything, but I've been finding it so difficult not to see you as someone who knows everything about me. The fact that you said you weren't sure has made me feel a lot more secure.'

Of course pastoral counsellors, like others in various occupations, have knowledge and expertise which helps make them competent. Their experience of working with people gradually builds up an understanding which is worth any number of books on psychology. At the same time each person is unique, with a particular set of circumstances which have led to the present position. The type of knowledge, therefore, which a helper has and demonstrates is not erudite psychopathology, which can be used to label people indiscriminately. A self-taught naturalist used to describe his idea of 'sweet power'. He meant by this the ability to stand in the countryside and to understand the relationship between the different forms of natural life, and the relationship to himself as the observer. This he felt was quite unlike the power gained from learning the scientific names of the flora and fauna, and then showing off this knowledge to others. His idea of 'sweet power' is a useful concept for the type of power which the helper has, and which he shares with his clients.[8] In Karen Horney's training manual she describes the client as 'the worker' and the therapist as 'the assistant'.[9] To apportion authority in the helping relationship in that way seems right, stressing as it does factors in the relationship which are less apparent in the terms 'counsellor/client' or 'therapist/patient'.

(Some therapists and counsellors use the term 'patient' and others 'client', largely depending upon the setting in which they work. Neither term is particularly apt in a book on pastoral counselling, where clergy might prefer the term 'parishioner'. Since in non-medical settings 'client' is the more common term, and this book is about counselling in general as well as about counselling in pastoral work, I use the term from time to time for convenience, variety and as shorthand, although not altogether happy with the connotations of the solicitor's office or even the brothel! It is difficult to convey the sense of individuality of persons in need in such a term which, of course, is never used in the counselling session itself.)

Because the counsellor is in a position to influence people, he not only needs to avoid gaining vicarious excitement through what is said, but he needs also to avoid encouraging those who see him to act out impulsively in ways which he himself would never do. The experiences and the fantasies of his clients will span the whole range of human experience, making soap operas, novels and even psychiatric text books appear insignificant to the real life dramas which are played out before him. Some of the problems he hears will be his own, while others may seem far removed from his own experience. Too much relish in the sensational, or too much self-consciousness about personally unresolved problems, can lead to difficulties in making an accurate assessment of what is said, of what should be explored, and of what he himself should say.

So I find myself returning full circle to the point at which I began, underlining the importance of self-understanding and self-acceptance for the counsellor, which in itself acts as a guide to how far he should be identified and involved with his client. The pastoral counsellor who is aware that the client's problem is also to some extent his own will be aware of the dangers of confusing himself with the other, and making unwarranted assumptions. Through self-knowledge he will be less tempted to project his own difficulties on to the client, and he will be less inclined to try and resolve them through another person. Yet he will not be afraid to explore a problem simply because it is close to his own. His insight into himself will enhance his understanding of the other. He will use himself more than most of his clients ever realize.

Awareness of these complex issues need not lead to disillusion or cynicism. Helping others must be personally satisfying if the job is to be done well. I doubt if pure altruism exists, and there is no shame in finding personal value through counselling work. Many of the relationships will bring pleasure and their own rewards. What is vital is that pleasures and rewards are not deliberately, or unconsciously, sought, especially in some of the more uncomfortable situations which inevitably arise in counselling, and to which I now turn.

Notes

1. H. Eadie, 'The Psychological Health of Clergymen'. *Contact* 41, Winter 1972, p. 2.
2. E. Rayner, *Human Development*. 2nd edn, Allen and Unwin 1978, p. 121.
3. Quoted by P. Roazen, *Freud and His Followers*. Penguin 1979, p. 151.
4. S. Freud, 'Recommendations to Physicians Practising Psychoanalysis'. In *Complete Psychological Works* (standard edn), Hogarth Press, 1951, p. 115.
5. H. Eadie, 'The Helping Personality'. *Contact* 49, Summer 1975, p. 6.
6. Ibid, p. 6.
7. H. Guntrip, *Healing the Sick Mind*. Unwin Books 1964, p. 87.
8. This theme is expanded in my article, 'Naming and Labelling', in *Contact* 54, 1976.
9. K. Horney, *The Barefoot Psychoanalyst*. Karen Horney Institute.

FIVE

Some Early Difficulties

The last chapter implies a tension for the pastoral counsellor between preventing his personal problems and conflicts from intruding, and yet using himself, his feelings and his thoughts as fully as possible in his work. The ability to keep in touch with his own reactions frequently provides insight into how the other person is feeling. Some reactions may be pleasant, others fairly neutral, while some will be distinctly uncomfortable, however experienced the counsellor may be. If he feels discomfort he can be fairly sure that the client is also experiencing it. Only where a helper continually experiences the same feelings with everyone will he need to question whether his reactions are saying more about himself than others, but such considerations will be looked at more fully in chapter 9.

Although the counsellor tries to be objective, he should not lose touch with the subjective feelings arising from the relationships with those whom he sees. Since there are few people who are relaxed and at ease in the first meeting, we shall consider some of the anxieties experienced by the pastoral counsellor with the new client (and with not-so-new clients), bearing in mind that these often reflect the anxieties of the clients as well. We shall also look at ways of responding in such situations.

The first point of anxiety, especially when about to translate learning into 'real' counselling, but also when about to meet new people, will often be one about competence. 'What sort of person am I about to meet? Will I like him? What will he make of me? What will his problem be? Will I be able to help?' As far as I know there is no way of avoiding such feelings. Each new person has to be faced. Anxiety about the unknown is more difficult than fear in the face of what is known. Once the interview is under way, especially if the helper can remain patient with himself, the anxieties will subside. However difficult a person is, the counsellor normally finds enough strength to get through, even if he needs to seek out some support afterwards. There is no shame in that. Most meetings will proceed more smoothly than anticipated, even though the new counsellor is almost certain to wonder if he is doing or saying the right things.

If the counsellor is worried, what do clients feel? Pastoral counsellors may already know some of those they see from other settings, such as when a parish priest offers counselling to a parishioner. This may not prevent the client having initial anxieties. 'What is counselling? What is expected of me? How can I express myself? What will he think of me? Will he criticize me? Will he think I'm making a fuss about nothing?' The experienced counsellor's initial anxieties soon subside once the session begins, but clients do not settle so quickly. The counsellor needs to be sensitive to their anxiety, perhaps encouraging it to be expressed, or easing it by creating an atmosphere of calm acceptance, and so making it possible for the person to come back and talk further.

Part of the counsellor's anxiety stems from his sense of responsibility. He is offering a service which carries with it expectations, although the client's expectations of the counsellor will differ. Different people will expect the counsellor to have answers, or to give advice, or to be an expert on human relationships, on spiritual matters or on mental illness. People are used to 'experts' because other professionals are often portrayed as such. The more desperate a person is, the higher his expectations. Unfortunately there are no answers available in the first few minutes, and perhaps not even in the first hour. As far as the counsellor is concerned the first meeting is an opportunity to formulate questions, in his mind, not answers: What brings this person now? What is he experiencing? How long has he felt this way? What has triggered off the present mood? What can I as a counsellor realistically achieve? What does the client want to achieve? How serious is he about using the help I have to offer?

The client too may ask questions, which can be difficult to answer. Does counselling work? What success do you have? How does it help? In answering them the pastoral counsellor can be honest, as long as he is tactful. 'I know that counselling frequently does help, which is why I am offering to see you. But I cannot guarantee it. In my experience it is more likely to help you if you can give it some time.' Openness about counselling from the very beginning avoids false promises or expectations, and also conveys a sense of partnership, by underlining the contribution which each person makes.

At other times people show their anxiety through different questions: 'What do you want to know? What do you want me to talk about? If you'ld ask me some questions I'll tell you what's relevant.' Similar feelings may be expressed non-verbally, with the client sitting looking intensely at the helper, obviously expecting him to take the initiative. At this point the counsellor feels responsibility being firmly placed on his own shoulders.

Whatever reply he gives, he should remember that this person has probably not met this type of interview before, and so naturally expects the 'expert' to first ask questions, and then to give advice. By sharing the responsibility with the client, the counsellor will help him to understand what it is about, and what his own role is.

'What would you like to tell me about yourself?'

'What do you think it would help me to know?'

'Try telling me what you are thinking and feeling, whether it seems relevant or not. There's plenty of time, and we can always meet again.'

'I know you would like me to ask you questions, but those would be my questions, and not necessarily what you want to tell me. Perhaps you have some questions you ask about yourself.'

Other people can be more direct in their opening words, indicating that they see the pastor as being like a doctor or a magician. 'I want you to get rid of my feelings of . . . I want some advice from you about . . . I want you to tell me what's wrong with me.' Such requests may appear flattering, and feed the pastor's wish to be seen as knowledgeable and powerful. Again his reply can begin to correct false expectations:

'I wish I did have some ready answer to give you, but I don't because every person is different. We want to discover what might be the right answer for you.'

'You know yourself better than I do, so it may take some time before I can begin to understand what it is that's troubling you.'

Such explanations, or others which fit the requests, are very important in the early stages, since they help a person to learn what can and what cannot be done, and something of what is expected of him. Reasonable answers might inform the intellect, but such rational statements do not always work, especially when ignorance is not the sole reason for anxiety. If the person continues to see the helper as a magician (albeit a wizard with a broken wand) such a false impression can be linked to the wish for a parent-figure who will make everything better. The 'child' in the client wants to rediscover in the helper the omnipotent parent who was lost in the disillusionment that accompanied growing up.

A compulsive eater had been seeing her doctor for a long time and the doctor had tried making some suggestions for controlling eating, which might have appealed to her conscious wish to eat normally. At one appointment the woman expressed her wish for someone to lock her up, control her eating, and stop her from making herself sick. The doctor then pointed out how she was sometimes asking to be looked after like a child, wanting someone there all the time, which would be the only way of stopping her from deliberately vomiting; yet at other times she rejected as unworkable the suggestions he had made to help her plan her eating. She was not able to take in what he was offering her, and so controlled him rather than allowed herself to be controlled.

There are some people who seem to begin with the right idea, but in fact may feel beneath similar wishes to be acted upon from outside. 'I don't think you are going to be able to help me. I know I have to help myself, and that you can't tell me what to do.' If there are hints of other expectations, such phrases can be taken up:

'I know that you rationally think that, but perhaps you still wish I could wave a magic wand and change things.'

'You said earlier that I couldn't tell you what to do, which is right, but you are obviously just as worried as when we started—perhaps you were wishing that I could have made things better for you today.'

Such responses reinforce the real responsibility which the pastoral counsellor has, which includes his refusal (unless absolutely essential for the safety of the client or others) to manage or direct another's life for him. His care and his concern is still conveyed in his manner, as well as in what he says, as he demonstrates his willingness to work within the limits of his understanding and experience. The client too is helped to see the part he has to play both in the counselling, and in the conduct of his own life.

Because he feels responsible, the pastor cannot help being anxious when he experiences feelings of complete helplessness. He may fear when a person is in real despair that he may make things worse, or that by default his inaction and inability to understand will drive a person to suicide. This helplessness will be felt most strongly with people who are very distraught, withdrawn and passive, or who talk about matters he does not comprehend. One reaction in this situation is to talk too much, or thrash around for something helpful to say. He may give advice prematurely or unnecessarily, or make links which are not thought out, and whose only dubious virtue is to fill the void.

At such times the old adage, 'Don't just sit there, do something', or the New Testament phrase, 'Speak the word only and I shall be healed', springs to mind. Actually the helper is more likely to be of use if he can reverse the adage, and tell himself at such moments, 'Just sit here. Don't do anything.' That will not prevent him feeling that he should never have decided to embark on pastoral counselling, that no one has prepared him for this, and so concentrate more upon his own discomfort than upon his client's. However, it is frequently the client's own sense of helplessness which he is sharing at that point, just as when he feels responsible it is the client's own desire for someone to take responsibility which impinges upon him. At such times the most effective support that he can give is to stay with the helpless feeling, waiting for the still small voice of calm to speak, as it will do as the level of anxiety drops in the counsellor or the client. The following example illustrates the value of 'just sitting there':

A curate had regularly seen one of his parishioners, Deirdre, during which time she had always shown considerable distress. On one occasion she arrived in a very desperate state. She was going to end it all; there was no way out; there was no point in living; and so it went on, her despair conveying itself increasingly to the curate. Recalling it afterwards, he could remember little of what Deirdre had said, or what he had said. What he did painfully remember was how helpless he felt, how he did not know what to say, and consequently how little he had in fact said. He thought that he may have encouraged her to express her feelings about wishing to 'end it all', but he was not even sure of that. He was so concerned for her safety, and for his reputation as a pastoral counsellor, that he felt immobilized. The only certainty was that at the end of the time with her he had said, 'There's nothing I can say which takes away the pain you are feeling. Perhaps when we meet next week, something might come then.' It was a desperate hope that he was expressing, not at all convinced within himself that next week would be any better. After Deirdre had left he sat dazed, unsure of how he should have dealt with what she was saying, and feeling that he did not want to do any more work that day.

After worrying about her and the session for at least an hour he decided that he had better, after all, get out and do some visiting. That afternoon he happened to meet in the shopping precinct one of those people who are always cheerful and full of life. Although the session remained on his mind, he forced himself to appear cheerful too, and then went on his way. All the following week the session came back to him, and he did not know what he was going to say, or how he was going to help.

The day and the time of their next meeting came, and to his surprise Deirdre entered the room looking more colourful, both facially and in her dress than he had seen her before. She was smiling, and she started by saying that she had wondered whether he would survive after last week. But she had seen him talking to someone and laughing, and realized that he had. She said that seeing him still cheerful had been a turning point for her.

It was a turning point for that curate too, because he realized that he had helped, not by saying anything of deep significance, but simply by surviving. We may wonder, of course, what would have happened had she not seen him in the shopping precinct; but other counsellors will confirm that 'simply' being there the next week would also have been a sign of surviving. The combination of that, and his ability to express Deirdre's sense of helplessness, had done more than anxious hyper-activity of words or actions.

Another aspect of his role is that the counsellor tries to understand everything that is said. There will of course be times when he does not understand and this may make him feel ill at ease. There are two types of understanding: the first is on the verbal level, of comprehending what is actually said, while the second is on another level, of understanding what it means. However experienced they are, counsellors will have occasions when they are unsure about the meaning of what is said. Inexperienced counsellors, however, may feel that they are not permitted to show that they have failed to comprehend the words being used, as if this shows they have not been listening properly. This is a false ideal, since no one automatically comprehends what is voiced, especially when nervous or confused people find it difficult to make themselves clear. In addition, however noble his intentions, the counsellor can drift off into his own concerns.

The helper who thinks he has to understand everything will feel anxious at such points. Yet if a person is not making himself clear he can say, 'I'm not sure I understand that—it may be my confusion, but if you could put it another way I'll probably grasp what you mean.' If a client says, 'You know,' and the counsellor does not know, let him say so. Even his drifting off can be covered tactfully by acknowledging, 'I didn't quite get that; it's me, I'm sure, but could you say that again?'

Turning to the deeper level of meaning, when the pastor understands the words and the sense, but not the significance, it is again possible to acknowledge this at the time, while storing away the words for later use as more material emerges. Often a phrase seems important, but its meaning unclear. It may fall into place later, or even after the session is over. Anything of real importance will always reappear again, sometimes in another form. Recording such thoughts and insight, even when it occurs later, reminds the helper to come back to it in later sessions when the opportunity arises. If the counsellor wishes to acknowledge at the time that he has heard, but not understood, he can say: 'I understand what you have been saying, but I'm not sure what that really means; it seems important. Perhaps it will become clearer as we go on.' As in all responses, much depends upon the tone of voice, and the manner of the counsellor. His still small voice will enable such comments to be made without causing embarrassment to the client.

There is a further aspect of not understanding, more likely to occur when counselling is more long-term. This is a feeling of being stuck, with either the client or the helper aware of going round in circles and getting nowhere. Since this can be a sign of resistance to change or to new material emerging, that particular discomfort is better examined in chapter 8.

At some point or other, perhaps at the first meeting, and very probably later, there will be discomfort for the pastoral counsellor, and even more for the client when silence falls and remains unbroken. Although silence can indicate a conscious or unconscious resistance to speaking about uncomfortable things, it is rash to put it down to that in the early stages. To some clients even the briefest of silences can be too long, and the counsellor needs to be alive to this, especially when he himself gets used to allowing longer pauses.

Silence can speak volumes. Before breaking it the counsellor can try and gauge what is being felt. I vividly remember conducting a group session in which, apart from my own unproductive interventions, silence reigned for an hour and a half. What was fascinating (and the members of the group said this when they were on speaking terms again the next week) was the way the silence moved in mood from embarrassment to anger, bewilderment to dejection, reflection to humour, with at times a deep sense of peace.

What therefore does the silence mean? Does the client not

know what to say? Does he know what to say but is too embarrassed to say it? Does he expect the counsellor to say something? Is it a natural pause while he thinks what he wants to say next? Is it a time for reflecting upon what he has said, or upon what the counsellor has said? Is it a battle of wills to see who will break the silence first?

When the counsellor can allow himself to tolerate the silence for a while, he may be able to gauge what it means. If he feels a need to break it (which in early sessions may be necessary) he can do it in a way which draws out the mood he perceives:

> 'You seem to be thinking hard—is there anything you want to share/find difficult to share with me?'
> 'You're not sure where to go from here?'
> 'You look puzzled, tense, upset, etc.'

It is not wise to allow silences to go on for too long when they seem uncomfortable to the client, although the counsellor who can give it just a little longer each time often finds that the client learns to accept it and break into it himself. Sometimes a person will comment, 'I don't like these silences,' or be even more direct: 'Can't you say something?' Explanations of what we are trying to do might help, such as: 'I want to let you go at your own pace—I'm not trying to play a game with you. I only keep quiet because I want you to have the chance to speak about what concerns you.' Or, if the person says at this point, 'I feel that you are expecting me to say something,' the helper can indicate that though in one way he is, he is not himself worried that there should be a silence, so long as it does not worry the client. If he wants time to think, that is all right. Particularly in early meetings the counsellor constantly and openly invites the trust and co-operation of the client.

In chapter 3 it was suggested that there are ways of reflecting back which can be used when there is a pause, and which encourage development of a theme. Early meetings can be easier in this respect than later ones, because the counsellor wishes to build up factual information, about the immediate situation, the recent history, and even the earlier history of the client's background. This need not be a psychiatric history, full of questions, even though it is necessary to build up such a history over time where counselling attempts to go into depth. By asking pertinent questions when certain subjects are touched upon, it is often possible to take a history without interrupting the flow of the sessions.

The temptation in early sessions is to use questions when a person is passive, in order to keep the interview running smoothly. When this happens the pastoral counsellor is in danger of setting himself up as the interviewer, or the doctor taking a history in order to make a diagnosis and/or prognosis. Questioning too early and too often creates a false impression of the counsellor's role, making the change to a free-floating atmosphere more difficult to achieve. As indicated in chapter 3, it is helpful to have some questions in mind, but it is better to ask only those which are related to what has been said. Asking questions out of context leads to a change of subject, helping the counsellor to find out what he feels he ought to know, but possibly at the expense of the client's priorities.

Many of the uncomfortable situations in counselling stem from the sense of responsibility a counsellor has, while at the same time being deprived of more tangible ways of giving help. Other pressures may also exist when a pastor has been asked to see a person at the request of a third party. We have noted already the natural wish to be a 'good' counsellor. Where he is employed by an institution or an authority which expects results, and may contain some individuals who are sceptical of the value of counselling, he may feel the need to demonstrate his worth to those who assume that his approach is 'the soft touch'. Where a person is referred by a third party, the pastor can feel pressure to show that the trust in him is warranted. There may be expectations from a person's relatives, or friends, who have arranged for the pastor to meet that member of the family. Where there is a high level of anxiety in a family, the pastoral counsellor may have to endure communications from them telling him what he should be doing, or indicating their concern about the progress (or lack of it) of counselling.

There are ethical questions here, as well as questions about technique. Unless a person gives express permission, the pastoral counsellor (like the confessor) is not in a position to communicate with others, however close or concerned they may be, even though he may wish to meet them to allow them to express their anxieties. In such cases tact and understanding of the dilemmas facing relatives and friends is called for. The client should be informed about communications that might otherwise be felt to be going on behind his back, and he will need to be assured that confidentiality is respected. If permission is given to pass on information, the helper needs to give due consideration to the effects of doing so. He may otherwise find himself as the 'go-between' for members of a family, obscuring direct communication between them.

Again, if counsellors are under this pressure, their clients may also feel it, and fear counselling, or perhaps even exploit it. The pupil who sees the school counsellor at the headmaster's request might fear that the counsellor is only there to enforce the Head's authority, and make him behave. The tutor who sends a student to a college counsellor might unwittingly create a situation where the student feels that the counsellor acts on behalf of the college. A helper may be seen as part of a punitive process (which in some instances, such as probation work or prison chaplaincy is partially true), or as a means of evading punishment, as if the counsellor is expected to be an advocate against other authority figures. A member of a family may feel he is only seeing the counsellor because his parents, or spouse have insisted upon it, using blackmail and threats that if he does not get help dire consequences will follow. An aged parent can feel that the helper has only come at the request of the children to 'put me in a home' or 'keep me quiet'.

In the face of these and similar pressures, the pastor or counsellor has to declare his independence and impartiality. It is not always enough to say it, and he needs to listen out for signs of further anxiety. In allowing such worries to be expressed he may incidentally expose family or institutional tension. Neither should the counsellor always take the client's side. Respect and acceptance does not mean getting caught up in the client's view of others. It will be difficult to be objective about the information which a person gives about other people; but counselling will only be of real value when a person can be helped towards recognizing his own contribution to the tense and difficult situations he describes. What has the teenager said or done that has provoked his parents into being so angry—perhaps he has been testing them out? Why does the girl who is constantly deceived by her boy friend stay with him, when experience suggests that he is unlikely to change?

One other 'third party' deserves brief mention. Overshadowing any counsellor's work will be his training, and the books he has read, which may appear to be putting pressure on him—books have a way of being felt as authoritative, telling him what he should be saying or doing. When he is being supervised, he will be aware that his trainer, or his peer group will be commenting on him when he reports his work. Particularly in sessions prior to presenting work in supervision, there can be tension between what he says spontaneously, and what he feels would 'look right' when he reports his case.

This leads to my final point. In a book which looks at technique and ways of coping with difficult counselling situations it is possible to give the impression that counselling is about game-playing, manipulation and counter-manipulation, or 'tricks of the trade', which, if it were true, would run counter to the wish to help others by being genuine, and helping them to be genuine. This would be a misleading impression, because the value of the person-to-person relationship is central to all helping work. The relationship is built upon and developed through the use of certain specific skills which are not obvious in normal social relationships.

There certainly is room for conflict here, which may lead the helper to feel the artificiality of certain aspects of the counselling relationship, leaving him wondering how to reconcile the role with his wish to be natural. I have already suggested that counselling is in some respects an artificial situation: there is intimacy, yet distance; there may be intense feelings, but they are feelings limited to verbal expression (i.e. non-physical); the perceptions of the counsellor made by some clients may be false, yet he may stay with them in order to understand the client better; instead of answering questions, the counsellor may choose to put them back to the questioner; he may express certain feelings such as pleasure or genuine amusement when both feel it, yet he will hold back other feelings (such as laughing at a person, anger and other 'negative' reactions); he sets boundaries of time, and yet may feel hard when he firmly sticks to them — these examples illustrate that counselling is not a normal social meeting, as many clients will be quick to observe, however much they come to value the opportunity to talk.

Against all this, the counsellor is also told that he must be 'real' and 'genuine' — two of the qualities which the research of Truax and Carkhuff,[1] for instance, has shown to facilitate change. He tries to be spontaneous, and yet at the same time tries to work correctly, applying the skills he has been taught. He may be taxed by clients who wonder why he does not talk about himself, and who may express some frustration that they know nothing about him (more likely to occur when they do not know a pastoral counsellor in other settings). Some even complain quite openly that they want a friendship. If he is at all human the counsellor can feel himself to be more depriving than giving.

Conflicts and discomfort such as here described are probably greater at the beginning than after a few years of experience. As Eugene Kennedy writes, 'The line between role and self gradually disappears.'[2] Technique becomes assimilated, more natural, more readily adapted to each situation, as the pastoral counsellor learns to feel free within his framework and his boundaries. As long as he is not obsessional, what appeared at one time as a set of hard and fast rules becomes a set of guidelines and reminders. With a secure base, his individuality begins to emerge in a way which does not intrude upon the client, but which enhances the relationship. The counsellor learns that technique which is used alongside care and compassion makes for better counselling, and he learns also to temper technique when it would clearly be counter-productive. Above all he comes to realize that much that is beneficial in counselling is also good human response, and that what at one time may have appeared to be a natural response is not quite so natural after all. When clients observe that it is a strange situation, he will find himself ready to agree, because it is unique. Counselling is not the same as friendship, as those who try to counsel their friends in a more formal way will soon discover. The warmth and genuineness of the counsellor is not the same as being 'friendly' — which in any case can be used to describe a shallow and superficial meeting of two people.

No amount of experience, however, prevents many of the feelings described in this chapter from being present at some time or another. They may not always be as disquieting, but they will always be around. If the helper forgets them, or denies them (as the partially trained person might be tempted to do in an effort to convince himself of his competence), the counsellor's work will be the poorer. It is through being able to monitor his own responses, especially the uncomfortable ones, that he is able to keep in touch with what others experience both in the relationship with him, and elsewhere with others.

Notes

1. C. B. Truax and R. R. Carkhuff, *Towards Effective Counselling and Psychotherapy Training and Practice.* Aldine Press, Chicago, 1967.
2. E. Kennedy, *On Becoming a Counsellor.* Gill and Macmillan, Dublin, 1977, p. 41.

SIX

Boundaries in Pastoral Counselling

Those who are asked to help, give advice, or to counsel frequently fall into one of two traps. The first, which is particularly tempting to those people who fill their week with frenetic activity, needing to prove to themselves and to others that they are useful, is to imagine that personal problems can be solved in a matter of minutes. Preferring to give advice than to listen, the helper only hears the bare bones of the problem before delivering a few 'comfortable words'. He probably allays his own anxiety more than that of the person who has approached him. His need is to 'do something' and to do it quickly.

The second trap is more common amongst those who have begun to learn the value of listening. In this case the eager helper spends one, two or even more hours at one sitting, listening, talking, hoping that with time a solution will present itself. What actually happens is very different. Helper and helped become more tired, and begin to go round and round in circles. The helper becomes more desperate to find a way through. Yet his tiredness and frustration makes this less likely the longer he goes on.

It is true that time heals, but the time which it takes to adjust to even the most acute situations has to be measured in weeks and not in hours. In all pastoral work the time which the helper can spend with a person in distress is necessarily brief, even if that time can sometimes be intense. The person in need will spend much more time in thought or activity on his own, or with others. We need therefore to consider how best to structure the time available for counselling.

There is a difference between formal counselling, and much of the work of clergymen, and of other professional and voluntary helpers. Counselling skills may be used in some settings where structured appointment times do not seem appropriate. When looking at boundaries this distinction must be borne in mind. I will look first at the more informal settings before examining the use of time in the more structured settings of formal pastoral counselling. Although the latter may not appear immediately relevant to some readers, I suggest that the principles involved may have some bearing on the less structured work of clerical and lay pastors, and that the way in which time is viewed by both the helper and the person being helped is one indication of more general attitudes, and even of personal needs.

Since personal difficulties are rarely resolved in one short meeting, this has implications for continuing contact. Every helper will have had occasion to visit someone, only to hear the complaint that such-and-such visited once, and never came back, or said he would call, and has not done so. There may be apparently good reasons for this: perhaps the caller felt that one visit was enough, or the busy clergyman or social worker had other demands and emergencies which filled the diary, making further visits more difficult. Those who are themselves so busy meeting others can easily forget that for the person whom they originally contacted, they might have been the only one to whom they could talk.

General pastoral work can therefore learn from the experience of counsellors, that there is value in making further appointments, fixing them ahead, and keeping to them. Reliability is one of the signs of caring. Even on those occasions when one meeting appears sufficient to resolve issues, the helper can always offer another time, if only to see how the person is coping. The offer will not always be accepted, but it should nonetheless be made.

Perhaps it would be easier to cope with what seem like the limitless demands of pastoral and other helping work if the pastor or helper could offer time, but time which had limits set upon it. We should not be ashamed to admit that there are some people whom we do not relish meeting, and the thought of an interminable time with them easily acts as a barrier to further appointments. Here again the limits which counsellors impose on the length of their sessions, and even the duration of their meetings, provide a model which can be used in other pastoral situations. The pastor can therefore suggest calling again next week, at a pre-arranged time, and add that he will be able to stay for a half-hour (or whatever time seems desirable and possible).

The frequency and duration of such visits, whether they are to his office or to a parishioner's home depend upon the circumstances. Where there is a bereavement regularly spaced visits provide a sense of structure for the bereaved at a time when their world may have gone to pieces. Although later visits may be arranged less frequently, the contact might be sustained for a period of months, since grieving is a long process. In highly fraught situations visits may need to be more frequent, though for a shorter duration. Supportive counselling, which differs from that type of counselling which explores and uncovers deeper feelings, often necessitates greater flexibility of time and frequency, although this does not mean limitless giving of time at any point.

Such arrangements will be worked out, however informally, by the pastor and the parishioner. Times must be mutually convenient. Certain times of the day might be avoided, especially when the chance of distractions in the home (e.g. the children coming home from school, shopping day) is increased. The formal counselling interview is in some respects much more comfortable for the counsellor (and the client) than many pastoral situations. We should not underestimate the additional stresses put upon the more informal·pastoral meeting which has to take place (it being the nature of much pastoral work to go into homes) on the client's own ground, where it is less easy to step back and view the immediate pressures surrounding him.

Practical arrangements such as those described have a stabilising effect in themselves on many of those who are distressed. They know that someone is there, that they only have to wait a few days before they can talk again. The reliability of this fixed point provides an anchor. Because this is so, the pastor should not alter arrangements lightly; if he has to, he tries to give due warning, and to make an alternative time. He should not let an arrangement go by default, at least on his part. If he has to alter appointments, or if holidays or other circumstances interrupt the regularity of visits, he should be alive to the possibilities of disappointment, and even allow such feelings to be expressed. The unreliable pastor will lose opportunities of helping others, and if he does not lose the people themselves, he will in all probability lose some of their trust.

Apart from the particular circumstances of the problem, and the other calls on a pastor's time, there is another factor which counsellors recognize influences the choice of frequency of meetings. The more frequently a person is seen, the greater the likelihood of dependence being created upon the helper. This is not in itself undesirable, and may be necessary for a short while. The less frequent the meetings, the smaller the opportunity to build up trust and to sustain continuity. Where dependency becomes a problem, the pastor can gradually space out the visits, making the changes clear, and still looking for signs of disappointment or anger.

Such boundaries help the client. They sometimes also help to protect the pastor or counsellor against that small, but significant minority of people who become very demanding, always finding every excuse to see and speak to the clergyman. Without wishing in any way to generalize, it is usually a woman who becomes fixated upon a man, who then proceeds to make life very uncomfortable for him—but it does happen the other way round, or in a homosexual attachment. The pastor who has made it a practice to arrange times ahead can use this to help limit the demands made upon him by pointing out (as patiently as possible) that 'perhaps we could talk about that at the time we have arranged to meet'. There are unfortunately no simple ways of handling these uncomfortable situations, but the setting of limits is certainly a necessary step in controlling the demands. Examples will follow from pastoral counselling which illustrate some of the other considerations involved with manipulative clients or parishioners.

With a better sense of the use of time—both its availability and its limits—the pastor, and also the person whom he sees, come to sense the possibilities of structure within the time-span of the meeting. The opening words often have significance—they may even act as the 'theme' for the meeting. The first half of the time can be used to encourage the person to expand upon his concerns, in ways described in chapter 3. Any comments, links or interpretations which the pastor wishes to make should be suggested while there is still time for the person to take them in and respond to them. The proximity of the end of their meeting can be pointed out a few minutes before either has to leave, and any feelings associated with the close drawn out. Although this is a somewhat idealized picture of a pastoral encounter, or a pastoral counselling session, it is a useful framework to have in mind.

There is one other major complication concerning a rather different type of boundary, which applies to clergy in particular, though it may be relevant to other helpers. Because the pastor has other roles, principally in the conduct of worship, the way he is seen and heard in these other settings influences the more individual pastoral care which forms another major part of his work. As preacher, the leader of worship, mediator of the forgiveness of sins, the minister of the sacraments, he may be seen as an idealized parent-figure by church men and women, or as a denigrated parent-figure by those who are antagonistic to the church. The boundaries of the one role cannot help overlapping the boundaries of the other.

For instance, a pastor may preach upon a particular moral issue, and in his congregation notice a parishioner whom he sees in his pastoral visiting. What will the parishioner be making of the sermon? As a preacher the pastor will put forward ideas more strongly than he would when accepting the failings of a person in a pastoral interview. He may be supporting in his sermon moral stands which the parishioner finds hard to make (avoiding sin or 'doing good' is not always a matter of will-power). He may be speaking of political or social matters which mean stating views which are in opposition to the parishioner's — so if that person happens to be narrow-minded, he may find it difficult to entrust other matters to a person whom he sees as disagreeing with him. The pastor cannot be the blank screen which the traditional analyst was. Likewise the pastor administers the sacraments, particularly the psychologically and emotionally powerful sacraments of communion and penance. I do not have space to examine the implications of this, although in passing I would observe that the giving of communion may carry with it associations of being fed as a baby by mother — as indeed the symbol of Corpus Christi (the pelican feeding its young from the blood of the breast) signifies. An example will illustrate the complications:

> Eve was seeing a pastoral counsellor who was also a priest. The priest visited Eve's church one day as a locum and gave her communion. At their next meeting Eve described how she had felt that she wanted to take the chalice from him at the communion and throw it down on the ground. The symbolism of this fantasy tied in remarkably well with something she had told him on another occasion: Eve's mother had told her that as a baby she constantly pushed away the milk which was offered her at the breast.

What does this mean for pastoral work, and in particular for counselling? Firstly it suggests that the pastor needs to remember not only what transpires in counselling interviews, but what the client says, and what he says or is seen to do in other situations. The pastor may find occasions when he can use this awareness with advantage in counselling situations.

Secondly it appears to suggest that the parish priest, or any other helper in a significant position, should be careful about engaging in counselling with a person who sees him in other roles. I do not personally subscribe to the dictum which comes from some analytic writers that it is impossible to meet in different circumstances. Counselling is not psychoanalysis, and the type of transference formed is normally much less intense. Furthermore, I believe that it is possible, given experience, to 'use anything', and that this includes distortions arising from outside situations. However, I concur with the caution, and suggest that where a pastor or any other helper is seen in more than one role, that the understanding of the relationship between himself and his client in counselling is more complex, and requires even finer assessment than usual.

There will be some readers who wish to develop the skills of more formal pastoral counselling, and I conclude this chapter with some examples of the use of time, and of the 'contract', which may not appear applicable to the less formal counselling opportunities described above. They do, nonetheless, point to some relevant issues about the respect for time, and are capable of wider application.

The structure of formal counselling will normally be one of a fixed session, a length of time which the counsellor works to, and often for an agreed number of sessions ahead. Although the duration of counselling can be extended if there is need and the counsellor has the space, a contract has advantages, not the least being that it helps to concentrate the issues. It also has implications for the handling of endings (see chapter 11). Time, duration and contract are, of course, not legal requirements, and every counsellor learns to temper firmness over the setting of boundaries with compassion and flexibility. It would be callous to push a person out at the end of an appointment, or at the end of a contract, where it is obvious that he cannot cope on his own. It would be uncaring not to give an extra appointment occasionally when time is available and when there is a genuine emergency. The pastoral counsellor should try to ensure that he has other resources he can call upon to offer his client if he is himself not in a position to meet such an emergency request. Although there are some dangers in acceding to such requests from some people, most isolated calls for extra help are made from genuine motives, when a person has reached the point of not knowing to whom else to turn. On most occasions there will be reasons external to counselling itself which give rise to such calls, but they are sometimes related to the previous appointment, where, for example, a chance remark by the counsellor may have unnerved the client, who has then to get in touch to check that all is still well.

Normally the correct timing of the session will help avoid such oversight on the part of the counsellor. He can, for instance, structure the time so as to allow a person who is very distressed to wind down, and leave in a relatively calm state, at least in outward composure:

> The session was coming to a close—there were only five minutes left. The pastoral counsellor noticed that the anger which Freda had been expressing had now turned to sadness. It was more noticeable in her eyes than in what she was saying. He wondered what he should do. Should he acknowledge the sadness, and perhaps open up the possibility of tears which might not be conveniently shed in the remaining five minutes? Should he leave it alone, and

perhaps lose the opportunity of reaching this aspect of her feelings? For a moment he kept quiet, weighing up the possibilities, until Freda pathetically smiled at him. His mind was made up. He said, 'It's nearly time to finish, but I'm aware how sad you feel. I'm hesitant about mentioning it with only a few minutes to go.'

Freda nodded, and began to cry in a restrained way. He went on: 'There's quite a lot of pain there.' She cried more openly, and he allowed her to do so for a brief while, before gently saying, 'It's difficult to stop there, but we must do so soon. Would you like a few minutes before you feel ready to leave?' Freda shook her head, dried her tears, and left, with the session ending only a few minutes over time. The next week she spoke about matters which showed that acknowledgement of her sadness had helped, because she had taken steps to help herself in the intervening period with some of the causes of it.

In addition to the sensitivity which the pastoral counsellor has about setting limits, he can use the feelings and reactions of his clients about the boundaries, to help them to understand more about themselves. Take, for instance, the start of a session. The client who is late may have indeed missed the bus, or as he says may have been delayed by a phone call just as he was about to leave home. The helper can take such excuses at face value. Persistent lateness, however, may be a sign of disorganization which affects other areas of life; at the same time the counsellor needs to be aware that excuses are sometimes rationalizations, and that disorganization may have other implications:

'I'm sorry I'm late. I'm not just late for you, I'm late everywhere.' The careers counsellor observed to George that he seemed to find it difficult to organize his life, and reminded him that that was one of the things he had initially complained of when coming for vocational guidance.

'It's not just that,' said George, 'I don't want to look as if I have to do what others want of me. I was late this morning for work too, because I'm blowed if I should do what the foreman wants.'

This helped the counsellor to realize that one of the

reasons why George could not hold down a regular job was that he was aware of being prone to comply too readily with the wishes of others, and so lose his independence. He compensated by over-asserting his independence, though always in a way which damaged others' opinions of him, and undermined his efforts to hold a worthwhile job.

'I'm late again.'
'You say that as if you think there's something significant about being late. Are you wanting to draw my attention to how late you always are?'
'That's true — I'm not sure of the value of coming here anymore.'

As this session went on Helen related how easily she got into a rut in her relationships with men, and how she liked relationships which were 'touch and go' — in more senses than one, as her counsellor pointed out. The counsellor's setting of times to meet was also seen as an attempt to control her and tie her down. She found it difficult to relate to any man who appeared to dominate her.

Lateness has many possible meanings: the helper may have kept the client waiting last time, or been on holiday, or altered an appointment, so that being late is a kind of 'tit for tat'; it may signify that what he has said, or failed to say or notice, made the client feel annoyed the last time they met; it may be a sign of anxiety about coming because it may mean talking about difficult subjects; it may mean that the client is dissatisfied with not getting very far, yet cannot tell the helper. Since counselling encourages the open expression of feelings, the counsellor watches out for hidden implications, in order to help them be expressed in words, rather than by acting out, whether it be coming late or missing a session. Because acting out may be a way of voicing criticism, the counsellor obviously needs to be prepared to accept criticism, otherwise he will probably let the misuse of time pass unnoticed, and with it an opportunity for greater honesty.

Turning now to the end of the session, certain situations also arise there which can point to less obvious meanings. Bringing up a subject which is provocative or exciting at the end may capture the counsellor's interest, and make him

unsure about finishing at that point. It can be a subtle
message from the client that he wishes for more time, and
cannot express this in any other way than by trying to claim
the attention of the helper. It may be useful to interpret such
(unconscious) ploys, when the counsellor can see this
happening. In the first example the pastoral counsellor did
not realize what was going on until afterwards:

A professional woman, Mrs Jones, saw a local minister at
her doctor's suggestion. There were some serious family
tensions which the doctor knew, but which the minister
did not. In his letter of referral the doctor had hinted at
these problems, but since they involved confidential
information about others he felt he should not divulge
them. The minister agreed, because he felt that he wished
to start from the beginning, and see what Mrs Jones was
prepared to tell him.

They had met a dozen times, with these hints known to
the minister, but not the details. There was little sign that
Mrs Jones wanted to tell him, though she referred from
time to time to a 'dark secret'. The minister tried to help
her explore what it was that made it difficult for her to tell
him, but to no avail. Then one day Mrs Jones started by
saying that today she had decided to tell him something
which he ought to know. The minister sat back, pricked up
his ears, and felt pleased that sufficient trust had now been
created to allow him to reveal the mysteries hitherto hidden
from him.

Mrs Jones said she would start at the beginning, which
for her was way back in the family history of those long
since dead. For forty-five minutes she went through this
history in detail, yet none of it seemed to touch upon
anything which would indicate why she was so depressed,
or upon the secret which was too shocking to be told until
today. She then said, 'It's very difficult for me to get it all in
today, could we go on now?' The minister was well and
truly hooked, and said that since this was his last
engagement of the day he would this once go on for another
forty-five minutes, if that would help. He was convinced
she would then tell all.

Mrs Jones took up her story from where she had left off,

and continued to cover the minute details of her early life for another forty-five minutes, but again with no hint of anything that could be described as dreadful. The minister was still none the wiser. He realized at this point that it had been a mistake for him to let her go on. After she had left, he saw how much this 'secret' had become a game between them. He began to recognize how she had been teasing him, and how she did this to men. The secret, which eventually came out, was of little significance compared to this point.

The counsellor who saw Karen began to see that the care and understanding he had shown her, which might in itself have been enough to help her over a crisis, was not sufficient, and that he had to help her with the difficulties over the limitations of the time he had available for her.

Karen's father, to whom she had been very close, had suddenly left home to live with another woman, turning his back on her and on the rest of the family. Naturally she was very upset, although she was not living at home, but sharing a flat with two other young secretaries. In her sessions with the counsellor Karen was fairly calm until the last minute, when he said it was time to finish. She invariably began to cry hysterically at that point, curling herself up into a tight ball in the chair, and arousing a lot of concern in the counsellor. At first he tried to ease the situation by reminding her that they would have to finish, but allowing her to calm down in her own time.

He then began to learn from other people that she was leaving him and casting herself upon them in a dramatic way, pouring out all her grief and anger, and clinging to those who offered to listen, for such a long time that they began to grow impatient with her. The counsellor realized that he was not shown much of the intense feeling himself, and that his own calm, accepting approach was missing something important.

After a particularly irate call from one of the girls in the flat he adopted a different approach. When the time drew near for the end of the session, he said, 'I think you may be feeling annoyed with me for saying we have to finish, when you would like to go on. 'No,' Karen replied sweetly, 'I'm grateful to you for listening to me.' 'But I still think you would like me to go on listening for longer,' he added, 'and perhaps you feel I turn my back on you as you feel your father has done.'

The next week Karen came very late for her session, saying she had forgotten about the appointment. The counsellor pointed out to her that it was most unusual for her to be late. He wondered if she felt annoyed with him for drawing attention to the limits. Despite her thanks at the time, she was perhaps still feeling resentful at having to leave.

It is not always possible to know why change occurs, but it was probably not pure coincidence that from that week onwards Karen ceased to take her troubles elsewhere, and began to make some adjustment to the 'loss' of her father.

There is little that occurs in the course of counselling that does not throw some light upon the fundamental difficulties of a client. The final example demonstrates how significant time and frequency of meetings can be to the client, and how reactions to the setting of limits illustrate underlying responses to other circumstances:

Mrs Lamb was a clergy wife, busy with all manner of 'charitable works', but unhappy at home. Her husband was not very generous with money, even though he had a private income. He would buy all the books and records which he wanted, but would brush off her own requests for things for herself. She found it difficult to ask him for anything more than the housekeeping. It emerged in the course of the first session that her father had never given her much encouragement, and was distant and stern, although her mother had often slipped her the odd five shillings when she was going out, and always showed an interest in her.

One week, between sessions, she 'phoned the pastoral counsellor to ask if she could have an earlier appointment, because she was feeling upset. Unfortunately the counsellor was not able to make it any earlier, and when she came at the usual time he also had to mention that he would soon be taking a break for his holiday, a few weeks ahead. He did not think to take up her feelings about the impossibility of arranging an earlier session, until the end of the time, when her tearful expression reminded him that he should have mentioned it. He said that she might still be disappointed in him, but Mrs Lamb said that it did not matter, which he took at face value. He thought afterwards that it would have been better to have said, 'I think it does matter to you,' because she looked quite angry as she left his room. He also realized that he had missed the significance of her saying that she had met someone at a dinner party who had confided to her that she too was seeing him. Mrs Lamb had realized that he saw other people, but actually meeting another woman client had made her feel jealous. Perhaps her wish for an earlier session had something to do with that chance meeting.

Opportunities missed in one session can often be taken up in another when the counsellor realizes what has been happening. The next time they met, his thinking was confirmed. Mrs Lamb said how angry she had felt last time because he had not given her any extra time, when he could see how upset she was. He only cared about her while she was there, and ignored how she felt between times. If he, like her, was really involved with helping people, he would soon realize that you have to be available to others whenever they need you.

The angry outburst enabled her to express her complaint, which was in itself helpful, since she was not one who could voice discontent openly. In the session that followed her outburst, the counsellor pointed out that although he had not given her extra time, she had replied 'It doesn't matter,' when he had suggested that she might be disappointed in him. She gave herself to others without setting limits, and this included giving way to her husband's whims. She obviously took this insight to heart, because the next week she began to make demands upon her husband, discovering to her surprise that if she asked he would respond, and that he was much more generous when asked than she had thought possible.

It was significant that when this counselling contract was coming to an end, Mrs Lamb told her counsellor that his work must be very demanding. Ironically she avoided being demanding herself, and in her helping work allowed people to make inordinate demands upon her. This counsellor's ability to respond to some of her demands, but to set limits on others, was not simply a means of avoiding over-involvement, and consequent emotional exhaustion, but was also the turning point which brought insight to Mrs Lamb, and the possibility of constructive action and change.

These examples come from the work of experienced counsellors, and illustrate the use of boundaries of time, and of the relationship between counsellor and client, with its 'transference' implications. They also show how counsellors with experience still find themselves missing signs from the client, which they are later able to take up. Using boundaries and transference in this way may not be typical of less structured pastoral work, and even in pastoral counselling such interpretations are not made without evidence. By scaling down the points illustrated in the examples. the pastor who uses counselling skills in his ministry will become more sensitive to the use of time, and the setting of limits, and understand how 'precious' some of the meetings become to those for whom he cares.

SEVEN

Supporting, Exploring and Confronting

From the description given so far of pastoral counselling it will be clear that the 'still, small voice' of the pastor cannot be equated with being a merely passive listener. Although he does not always say much, when he does speak what the counsellor says, and the way he says it, can have a decisive influence upon the eventual course of a person's life. While it is the client who provides the main substance of the interview, the counsellor makes an important, if less vocal, contribution.

The nature of this contribution casts doubt on the validity of a phrase often used of counselling: the term 'non-directive'. The expression originates with Carl Rogers, who uses it as an alternative to 'client-centred' counselling. But the two terms are by no means synonymous. Presumably Rogers means by both phrases that the counsellor does not give advice, nor introduce his own agenda. His task is to listen carefully, to accept what is said, to show warmth and genuine concern, and to reflect back accurately what he hears from his client. To call this 'client-centred' is fair enough, but it is misleading to call this 'non-directive'. Since every interview has a beginning and an end, the counsellor is directive about time. The presence and the personality of the counsellor impinges upon the client, and therefore influences what a person chooses to reveal. If the counsellor chooses to remain passive and simply listen, his silence will in itself evoke various feelings (probably of anxiety). Yet as soon as he intervenes, he in some way alters the direction of the interview. He chooses to reflect back one phrase, yet not another, or to give particular stress to one feeling, and not another. When he reflects back, he selects which of the client's words he wishes to use (unless he were to repeat everything, which would make nonsense of the interview). When Rogers is seen on film with the client 'Kathy' there is a point early in the session where he adds words which were not said. He is quite correct to do so, because he makes central a difficulty which Kathy avoids; but in doing so he clearly steers the interview in a particular direction, the problem of relationships 'with men', and not just of relationships generally.

It is impossible to avoid imposing some direction, however slight. It is better to admit that this happens, and to exercise care in directing, than to believe in the myth of non-directiveness. There is nothing strange about this, since it occurs in all conversations. One person speaks, the other responds, and provides a cue which is taken up, missed, contradicted, etc. Each offers direction to the other. Exactly the same happens in the counselling interview. The client begins, while the counsellor listens. The counsellor takes up what he believes is important to the client, and the client responds by agreeing, or rejecting, by accepting part of the reply, or by changing the subject. In an open relationship both parties take initiative, listen to each other, respond, agree and disagree.

There are, of course, differences between the counselling interview and an ordinary conversation. The client is encouraged to do most of the talking, to express himself spontaneously and openly, to avoid holding anything back. The counsellor says far less, and when he speaks he weighs his words carefully, not only to show that he has understood, but to ensure that what he says is not taken the wrong way. The counsellor also chooses how he wishes to intervene, depending upon what will help a particular client. Part of his own responsibility is to decide when to support, when to explore, and when to confront.

Where a helper reassures or supports a client, he generally does so to suppress anxiety, and foster the positive aspects of the client. When he intervenes to explore or to confront, he is aware that he might provoke a certain amount of anxiety, and possibly pain, but he does so believing that this will help more in the long term. Interventions can be used either way, to suppress or uncover.

In chapter 5 I suggested that in the early stages a new

client will be helped if we can explain what is expected in the interview, if the person seems anxious. Let us now suppose a client who is used to counselling, and has not needed such guidance before. Today he starts by saying, 'Where shall I begin? I don't know what I'm going to talk about today.' The pastoral counsellor can take this up in one of a number of ways:

1. He can suppress the anxiety by saying, 'It can be difficult sometimes; it doesn't seem to have been so before, but don't worry. I guess there are some things on your mind.'

2. He can explore the anxiety: 'You're feeling anxious. What do you think the difficulty is today?', inviting the client to think about it.

3. If he is aware of an explanation, he can explore and confront: 'You mentioned at the end last time that you wanted to talk about sex. Perhaps now you're here it's not so easy to do that.' Here he suggests a reason for the hesitation, and more openly confronts what he thinks might be a block in the person's thinking.

Or consider the different responses to a silence. We have looked previously at ways of breaking an awkward silence, such as introducing the topic mentioned before the pause. The silence itself can be explored, starting perhaps with the feelings evoked by it in the helper. A third way chooses to heighten the anxiety by allowing the silence to continue:

Mark said rather hesitantly: 'I have these dreadful thoughts. I'm not sure I want to talk about them.' He lapsed into silence. The helper had a good idea that they were thoughts about herself, but she felt that this was one occasion when Mark should own his feelings himself. She allowed the silence to continue, and the atmosphere became quite tense. The man shifted in his seat, knowing what he could say, but unable to do so. After a few minutes he blurted out, with considerable anguish, 'I try hard not to think them.' The helper quietly said, 'But they are there all the same.' There was another pause, briefer this time, before Mark again exploded with anger and said what he was thinking. When he finished he seemed relieved, and the helper began to help him understand why the thoughts were so frightening to him.

She could have handled it differently, but she knew that Mark could tolerate the tension, and that if she had given him any excuse he would have put off saying what he did. With a different person she might have said, 'Thoughts are only thoughts, they don't harm anyone. It's up to you whether you want to tell me or not.' She could have asked what made it difficult to express them. Choosing to maintain a high level of tension with Mark she helped him express them with their true force when he eventually spoke.

Even asking questions can be used to support, explore or confront. A client speaks of a week which has had its ups and downs, and then passes into silence. Should a question be necessary, the pastoral counsellor can either ask about the ups, or the downs, supporting or exploring. He can ask about both, leaving it to the client to choose which to take up. We should notice too that even in seeking more factual information some questions may focus on embarrassing subjects, and that there needs to be caution with some people about asking questions which are too forthright:

An eager-to-learn social worker had been on a day's course on sex therapy, and had learned that a full history of sexual attitudes and behaviour was essential, since some clients had misinformation about sex which needed to be clarified so that a programme of re-education could be begun. He recognized the importance of this soon afterwards, when after a number of unproductive sessions a couple from a different ethnic culture explained that their religious beliefs forbade them touch each other's genitals in foreplay. He understood rather too late why his attempts to help them had so far got nowhere.

His next client who had a sexual difficulty gave him the opportunity to set all that right, and to take up the advice about taking a full sexual history. The young man was quite naturally somewhat hesitant about talking about sex. He seemed to want to talk about his most recent unsatisfactory relationship. Eager to do his job properly this time, the social worker kept questioning the young

man about his first sexual experience, because he felt
details were important. He proceeded to ask similar
questions about the next relationship. But the young man
was urgently hurrying on, wanting to know what was
wrong with him. This urgency seemed to throw some light
on his problem which was premature ejaculation. The
social worker suggested that in his anxiety to get on he was
unable to relax. He took up one of the young man's phrases,
about being a 'bull in a china shop'. But the client did not
come back for a second appointment, and it became clear
to the social worker that he too had not been able to relax.
The questions he asked, which were too clumsy and
provocative, made him just as much a bull in a china shop.

Reflecting back is a common way of intervening, and can
take up phrases which indicate progress, thus being
supportive, or take up phrases which indicate concern, thus
choosing to explore tensions. How would you choose to reflect
back to the following opening?

'I've had a much better week at the office. I was telling you
how difficult it was to do the accounts, and how I couldn't
get down to them because I was afraid the senior partner
would find mistakes. But this week I got on with them,
finished them, and they were perfectly all right.

'I was quite pleased too about the way I coped with
tension I felt in the lift on Tuesday, despite the boss's
secretary being there. I had a good weekend too. I went out
for a meal with friends, and Jane was there—I've told you
about her—and she seemed pleased to talk to me for once.
I'm not sure whether to go round and see her again this
week—I could dig up some excuse to call, like wanting to
borrow a book.

'I've been waking up early this week, just when I'd given
up taking the sleeping pills. I did want to keep off them,
but things don't seem so good since the weekend.'

There are a number of possibilities. The counsellor can reflect:
'It's been a good week on the whole,' or 'You've been feeling
more confident this week,' or 'It sometimes helps not to come
off drugs too quickly'—remarks which are supportive and
may lessen anxiety, at least temporarily. Alternatively he

could take up some of the more thorny issues: 'You seem
excited, but also worried, about meeting Jane again,' or
'Waking up early still worries you,' or 'You seem to feel tense
when you meet certain women'. Yet a third way is to reflect
back both the pleasant and unpleasant aspects of the week,
although bearing in mind that the emphasis given to one
phrase may be the cue for the client to take up that issue.

Counselling obviously moves between supportive remarks
and those which can heighten the problems; with many
people both styles are used. In some cases, one style will be
more appropriate, although even then the pastoral counsellor
should remain alert to the need to move from one to another.
Supporting can sometimes give enough strength to a person
to help them move into more exploratory work, while working
with the anxieties can necessitate a retreat into supportive
work. The following two examples demonstrate such a shift
in direction:

> A young church member had gone away to college, but was
> home every weekend, and frequently saw his minister on
> those occasions. In the first term he was obviously clinging
> on to home and church, and the minister concentrated
> upon supporting the young man, who was always on the
> verge of leaving college. Each essay, each lecture, each
> failed relationship made him feel very low. Progress was
> slow, but in the second term he began to show signs of a
> different side of himself. He said at one meeting that when
> he was at home, he would sometimes swear if he dropped
> something. His parents would laugh at him in a playful
> way, as if he was a little boy who did not know what he
> was saying. He seemed quite angry about this, and it
> appeared that any efforts at home to be more independent
> were humoured. He mentioned that his parents worried
> about him. The minister realized that here was a stronger
> character than he had at first spotted. He therefore changed
> the tenor of his remarks, ceasing so much to concentrate on
> supporting the efforts to stay at college, and instead
> pointing out to the young man that he seemed to be saying
> that his parents were reluctant to let him go, and that he
> found himself playing along with them so as not to offend
> them. As these ideas were drawn out, there was quite a

change in the descriptions the student gave of his feelings at home. He talked now of being swamped by his parents, whereas previously he had felt stranded when away from them. He had in the first term feared his parents dying while he was away, but now he began to say that he would miss them, of course, if anything happened to them, but that he could live without them. What had started as a supportive relationship, aimed at helping the student to stand by his efforts to stay at college, turned into one in which the minister helped the young man look at issues which made it difficult to leave home.

Nancy had found her counselling very helpful, and seemed to value the opportunities it gave her to think about herself. She was obviously making advances in her job by asserting herself more. The probation officer was pleased to see how she was exploring past and present relationships in the sessions. However, after a while the valuable progress made seemed to take a turn for the worse. Nan was rejected by a man she had tried to get to know at work, and to whom she had presented herself in a very facile way. She came to her appointments with so many thoughts in her head that there was never enough time to explore them, and there were signs of considerable confusion. She denied that she was at all worried, and said how much she liked to talk about herself. She was behind with her work, and was using the time at the office to write her life history. It seemed as if what had started as useful exploratory work had turned into a very introverted, narcissistic, and unreal view of her life, with signs that she was in danger of losing her job and her grip on reality.

The probation officer therefore promptly changed her approach, and became much more directive. She told Nan that she could see how she valued thinking about herself, but that her thinking was taking up so much of her time that she was putting other aspects of her work and life at risk. She advised her to try and put her life history on one side for the time being. She helped Nan to structure her day so that she was able to give more time to the firm and think less about herself. The counselling which had started by trying to foster insight was obviously no longer working to Nan's advantage, and this change of approach was clearly indicated given the constraints on the probation officer's time and skills.

The interventions of the pastoral counsellor and other helpers so far considered can therefore be used in these two ways, to support, and to explore the anxieties. There is another method of intervening which does not form part of supportive work, since it clearly can generate some anxiety. We call this 'confrontation', where the counsellor deliberately draws attention to something which is being avoided. He tries to make the person more explicit and honest in expressing thoughts and feelings. For example:

Client:	This girl came round to see me last night. We talked all night.
Counsellor:	You just talked?
Client:	Well . . . yes.
Counsellor:	You mean 'no'?
Client:	Mm. Well, you see, whenever she comes to talk to me she always finishes up by wanting to go to bed with me.
Counsellor:	And it's just her that wants it?
Client:	Well, no, but then I feel awful about it the next day.
Counsellor:	But you might enjoy it too?
Client:	I suppose I do, if I'm honest.
Counsellor:	It seems quite a complicated situation.

Client:	My friend was going on and on about her aches and pains, how she'd been to see the doctor, and he was no good, how unsympathetic her husband was; on about her children—and there was me trying to rush to catch the bus into town, and I was getting more and more fussed—so I nearly said to her—well, no, what I actually said was . . .
Counsellor:	What you *nearly* said was . . .?
Client:	No, it doesn't matter.
Counsellor:	You can say it, she's not here.

Client: Well, what I wanted to say was, it's all bloody
           well for you to go moaning on, but what about
           me? You don't know the half of it, you don't
           know what a bloody mess I'm in . . .

Finally, some examples of the counsellor confronting, taken
out of context, but illustrating other ways in which
confrontation is used:

'Every time I suggest something you tell me I'm wrong, as
if you're afraid of letting me get close to what you're really
feeling.'
'You often talk about your children but you never mention
your wife.'
'You look as if you want to cry, but can't let it go.'

I have noticed in conducting role-play exercises in counselling
training how often the person who plays the part of the
helper avoids taking up painful remarks and hints which the
person playing the client has been asked to drop. There
seems to be some fear of exploring and confronting, perhaps
because listening and understanding has been stressed so
much, and perhaps because there are fears of hurting the
client. In fact the client has come to the helper because he is
already hurt, and exploration, or even confrontation, may
enable the hurt to be shared, this in itself bringing some
relief. For example, in response to the last short example
above, a client said, after breaking into profuse tears, 'That's
better: I haven't cried for years; I've been fighting it back all
this time.'

But confrontation is not a means of trying to catch a person
out, of making him appear small, or of punishing him. If a
helper is particularly aware of angry feelings towards a client,
he needs to exercise great caution in using such an approach.
All helpers learn to recognize that people have defences, and
that defences serve a purpose, as we shall see in the next
chapter. If there is insufficient rapport between counsellor
and client, confrontation may drive the client away. Eugene
Kennedy warns against the improper use of this type of
intervention. 'It is not a hit-and-run operation. It is not a blunt
instrument . . . [It is not] clubbing the other person through

immediate and massive direct attack . . . A search and destroy expedition against the defenses of others is a sad but unfortunately popular form of confrontation . . .'[1] Neither, would I add, is it the iron fist in the velvet glove, but rather the 'still small voice' which speaks more clearly than the earthquake, wind and fire.

In the hands of the clumsy counsellor confrontation is a dangerous weapon. In the hands of the skilful counsellor it is like a surgeon's scalpel, delicately opening up areas of pain, or shame. Even then the counsellor is ready to stem too great a flood of hurt or feeling. Firmness and sensitivity go hand in hand with flexibility, as the pastoral counsellor gauges the possible reactions of his client to his interventions.

There are often early indications in the manner of a client, his history, and in his presentation of his problem, which give clues to the helper as to the most appropriate approach to use — and indeed to decide whether counselling is a suitable approach at all. Those who are obviously bizarre in their thoughts, or are so disturbed that they make the counsellor feel more than usually uncomfortable, are likely to need an approach which is solely supportive. Such people may appear to believe that all is well with them, when it is obvious to the counsellor, and to others, that it is not. They may have very poor relationships, and may show little sign of having related even to one person properly (even if adversely). They are equally unlikely to relate to the pastor sufficiently well to make use of a counselling approach which aims at exploring problems. If such people have experienced difficulties for a very long time, especially in coping with normal fluctuations in circumstances, or if they speak of emotional difficulties which have been with them for many years, the pastor will indeed be cautious about suggesting counselling at all. This does not prevent him from supporting such a person through a crisis. The amount of time he can give in a busy ministry is unlikely to bring about a real change, although in some cases referral to a psychotherapist might be appropriate. If in addition to such long-term problems a person talks in a confused way, jumping from topic to topic, with ideas clearly out of touch with reality, referral to a general practitioner or a psychiatrist is probably indicated.

When faced with such people, the counsellor is often aware

of a type of discomfort in himself which bears little resemblance to that which he feels with someone who is in deep distress, but is only temporarily incapacitated. Without usurping the role of the psychiatrist, he can ask questions to see how long the feelings and thoughts have been present, whether there has been previous medical and psychiatric treatment, or whether this is a more immediate crisis which has been preceded by more normal experiences and reactions. If the pastor chooses to be a support to those who are seriously disturbed, greater flexibility of time might be necessary—a few minutes on some occasions, longer periods at other times, with greater frequency of contact sometimes necessary. The helper tries to support the defences of the disturbed person against fears of internal impulses, or external pressures, or against the harsh voice of an over-strict conscience—any of which might threaten to overwhelm the 'self' at the centre of a person.

Encouragement and praise is therefore given for every positive action, or sign of coping. Reassurance may not always be enough, and the pastor may have to be more directive, or give advice, or help decisions to be made which are realistic and responsible. He may even have to manage the person's environment, or call upon others to assist in this task. If the person feels threatened by mention of doctors, psychiatrists or others (and some people have had experiences of professional help which cannot merely be dismissed as paranoid) the pastor has to be careful how he suggests referral, and how he handles the transition from himself to another helper.

Even with people who are not so disturbed, there is an art in making a referral, especially when first suggesting it. There may not be particular anxieties about seeing another person, although referral itself may be felt as a rejection— especially if the client has specifically approached the pastor, or has been shunted from pillar to post in the past. If too much resentment is aroused the person referred may not be so co-operative with the next helper. Referral inevitably means repeating one's story, and if a person has had to pluck up courage to tell it once, he may shrink from the thought of having to tell it all over again. Nevertheless, pastors and counsellors are not omnicompetent, and some referrals have to be made. The earlier it can be done, or at least mentioned as a possibility, the less likelihood there is of feelings of rejection, and the more time there is to allow reactions to be expressed, especially to pick up residual feelings which are not openly voiced. The helper may have to explain why a referral is necessary, but such explanations must avoid unnerving the client, especially when they stem from the helper's recognition that he is not the right person to handle this client's situation.

As one who receives more referrals than one who makes them, I am sometimes aware of the lack of forethought and consideration in the referral. The person who comes to me from another immediately voices concern which could have been talked over at the point of referral. The following example is a composite statement which, though fictional, illustrates the most common errors in referral:

'. . . I was told to come and see you (1). I don't think Mr Smith had time to see me (2). I don't know why I'm here — is there something really wrong with me? (3). I never thought I'd have to see a psychiatrist (4). What am I to do? (5). Do I have to start all over again? (6) . . .'

It is not difficult to see how this referral could have been handled better.

1. The client comes to see me to please Mr Smith rather than because he sees the benefit of help for himself.

2. He sees the referral as a rejection, and rationalizes what is perhaps an anxiety that the person referring did not wish to go on seeing him.

3. No reason has been given for the referral, leaving the client to imagine the worst about himself.

4. This is confirmed in his statement about seeing a psychiatrist. The person referring has not clarified my true role.

5. No explanation has been given of what to expect of counselling. What started perhaps as an informal approach

to Mr Smith has become a more formal process with consequent anxieties.

6. Starting again and not being sure what the counsellor already knows could have been made easier had the person referring asked the client's permission to communicate the bare facts of the difficulty, in order to break the ice.

Turning now to those who can use a counselling approach which explores and encourages insight, and where confrontation might be appropriate, the pastoral counsellor will again look for signs of suitability in the first interview. There should be indications that such people have functioned adequately before the onset of the present crisis; that they have achieved some success in relating to at least one other person, and in their capacity to work. The pastoral counsellor will want to see signs of a conscious wish to change, although such improvement and change should not be expected to come about only through external means—through a belief in a magical answer, or expectations that it is others who must change. This counselling approach looks for a client with the ability to keep in touch with what he experiences and feels, and some ability to put this into words. The client will need to show some capacity to relate to the counsellor, and to be sufficiently co-operative to give thought to what the counsellor says. He should show some recognition of his effect on others, and theirs on him, and be sensitive to what others feel. Finally he needs to be able to accept the length of time that it might take for change to occur, which means in effect that he will have to bear with his problems in the time it takes for counselling to begin working upon them. What an ideal person. With such clients counselling should not be necessary! This list of 'virtues' is only, of course, a catalogue of pointers to the type of person who can benefit from this particular pastoral approach. There are few who will fit it completely.

There are other people who ask for help, who are neither bizarre, nor seriously disturbed, yet who do not meet these conditions. They include the very quiet, passive, non-verbal person. Supportive counselling might help them, as will more active forms of intervention, such as behaviour therapy, or social skills training. However, in the average pastoral ministry many of those who make initial contact can be helped by using the counselling approach described in these chapters. Although some people may find difficulty at first adapting to what the pastoral counsellor can offer (it being unlike other forms of 'expert' help), the helper who can be flexible will often in a few appointments create a working relationship in which insight and exploration gets behind the presenting problem, in a move towards greater self-understanding. With the self-knowledge which comes through deeper exploration, the pastoral counsellor offers the opportunity for more than surface change and immediate relief; and this is more consonant with the theological dimensions of pastoral care and counselling, in which the movement towards wholeness is indeed in harmony with the religious view of man.

Notes

1. Eugene Kennedy, *On Becoming a Counsellor* Gill and Macmillan, Dublin, 1977, pp. 128-33 passim.

EIGHT

Meeting Resistance

If pastoral counselling aims to help a person discover more about themselves, the counsellor has to learn how to enable people to overcome the barriers they often set up against seeing themselves more fully. This and the next chapter develop this aspect of the work, an understanding of which is essential for anyone who wishes to practise that type of counselling which goes into a person's life more widely, more deeply, and perhaps earlier, than the immediate difficulties initially presented.

Barriers there will almost certainly be, and it is tempting to the helper to try and bulldoze them down in an attempt to reach further. But counselling should not become a battle between counsellor and client. If the image of battle has any value, it more aptly describes a struggle going on within the person who has asked for help. Although the conflict will not always be clear, there is often awareness of a struggle, well described by St Paul amongst others (Romans 7.23), between one side, which consists of conscious, reasonable feelings and values, and another side, less tangible, but often stronger, containing frightening, exciting or punishing emotions and thoughts, which threaten to break through and take over. The person asking for help often wishes the counsellor to take sides, to support his reasonable, conscious self, and to help him get rid of the unwelcome, intrusive feelings. He wants to restore the *status quo*, to get back to 'normality', as it was indeed felt to be before.

On the other hand the pastoral counsellor, while tempted to do this, knows that he will serve the other better by not taking sides in such an obvious way, and that his task is to help the person, first to recognize, secondly to accept, and thirdly to understand the reasons for the alien emotions and thoughts. The counsellor, as is appropriate to his theological stance, is a mediator. He wishes to see both sides, and to help the client to bring together the forces which are in opposition. What appears threatening to the client can, in fact, contribute to a greater sense of completeness. 'Bad' feelings may not turn out to be so bad after all; they can at least be brought under stronger control rather than pushing them down. They may even be turned to advantage and towards greater good. This is no simple task. The embattled person does not wish to face the 'bad' side, which is felt to be damaging, dangerous, immoral or harshly critical. He puts up barriers, sometimes even unaware that he is doing so, to the attempts made by the helper to bring all sides of him to light. He would prefer the counsellor as an ally against the enemy within. The reasonable side of the client is afraid of what will ensue if the opposing forces are given expression—often fearing the expression will turn into action. The 'enemy within' (also part of the person, and with a 'mind' of its own) similarly fears what will happen if brought into the open. Employing our image of the battle, the forces within are afraid that the counsellor is a fifth columnist, who will force an unconditional and absolute surrender. Such an analogy sounds dramatic, and it is no doubt over-simplified, but it conveys the sense of struggle which goes on within people. Sometimes people talk of themselves as 'schizophrenic'—not an accurate use of the term, but nevertheless a word which conveys for them their feeling of being two people fighting each other.

The barriers referred to are not in themselves 'bad'. Psychologists call them 'defences', and their value can be seen if we use a different analogy. In transplant surgery one of the major problems is the body's rejection of alien tissue; drugs are necessary to keep at bay the natural defences of the body, but at the same time they must not render the body so defenceless that there is risk of infection. The mind has similar defences, which protect a person from the dangers of severe conflict or great shock. An obvious and familiar defence is the numbness which can follow a sudden shock, as if feelings are temporarily anaesthetized. This may enable a person to function semi-automatically. Following a road accident, a by-stander may be able to summon aid, give assistance, and show remarkable signs of coping. It is only later that the full effects are felt, when shaking, or other discomfort is experienced. At that point the person begins to go over the incident in his own mind, or will tell others, sometimes over and over again, until eventually the experience can be recalled without such a deep sense of horror. Counselling frequently assists those who have suffered similar shocks, by giving them an opportunity to speak about events and attendant feelings, sometimes over and over again, until they become less threatening.

The defences which are employed in the face of unpleasant or shocking thoughts and feelings are far more extensive than numbness. The pastoral counsellor learns to recognize these defences from the way people describe themselves and their attitudes. He will also see them at work in the interaction between himself and the client — where the defences are given the technical name of 'resistance'. His knowledge includes the understanding that defences serve a useful and natural purpose. Indeed for all of us some defences are essential. Supportive counselling, as described in the last chapter, deliberately reinforces defences as long as they are working relatively satisfactorily. In the type of counselling which tries to uncover inner conflicts, defences and resistance are handled by helping the person comprehend why they are necessary. By demonstrating the reasons for defences, a person becomes more ready to lower them, inch by inch, as it becomes safer to face the feelings which they mask. Here again we see the need for the pastoral counsellor's interventions to be framed in an atmosphere of 'gentle stillness'.

In this chapter various defence mechanisms are reviewed, together with signs of resistance in the counselling process. Some of the reasons for defences will also become apparent. Defence mechanisms have acquired technical labels in analytic literature, and the terms are used here simply for convenience, and communication in supervision. They will not always be expressed so technically in the pastoral interview. Some of the terms, such as 'projection' or 'denial' are known and understood by some of those who have read a little psychology, but the language used by the counsellor should always be at the client's level. One complication in describing defences in such technical terms as I do is that it gives the impression of neat pigeon-holing; in practice defences often overlap and defy neat categorization. What is important for the pastor and counsellor is the ability to decipher the specific forms of defensiveness. He need not trouble overmuch about precise labels.

Most defences are ways of trying to cope with thoughts, feelings or memories which are too threatening to admit fully into consciousness. *Splitting,* for instance defends against ambivalent feelings towards one person, or one object. Like projection it is believed to be a defence which operates very early in infancy, where it is strictly speaking then a natural phase of development. The baby has none of the adult's more balanced view of the world. He experiences good feelings, and bad feelings. The good are related to a mother who is available when wanted, who smells good, tastes good, and feels good. The baby also has bad experiences, when mother is not there, when she is cross or impatient, when she cannot feed the baby fast enough, or when she is preoccupied. The baby is not yet aware that good and bad experiences are related to the same person, and so develops a split image: there is a good mother who is associated with fulfilment, and a bad mother who is associated with frustration. In normal development these two images are brought together into one. The child learns that those who bring satisfaction can also be frustrating, and that those who frustrate can also sometimes satisfy. When development proceeds satisfactorily, the good image is strong enough to contain the bad image, and good feelings can contain the fear of bad feelings. Theology and mythology contain many symbols of the primeval or ultimate conflict between good and evil which underline the significance of this as a basic human problem.

No one develops perfectly, so it is not surprising that traces of splitting are evident in all of us, though in some people it is more obvious than in others. Conversations between people sometimes reveal black-and-white attitudes—the Russians are warlike, the Americans want peace; the Labour party is the party of care, while the Conservative party is the party of greed. In families mother may be seen as generous, and father as mean; in parishes the vicar may be described as a traditionalist, while the new young curate is praised for having all the new ideas. In schools some teachers will be idolized, while others are seen as monsters. In groups with shared leadership, one leader can be seen as helpful and the other as obstructive, although another group may see the same two leaders in completely the opposite way. There is sometimes an element of truth which appears to substantiate such perceptions, and those who are split in this way are on occasion happy to collude with it, particularly if they are seen as being on the 'good' side.

In pastoral work helpers will come across people who use this defence by seeing two or more helpers simultaneously, dividing what they have to say, so that one helper is given one story, the other a different one. Such a person may flatter the one and denigrate the other, provoking and actually promoting feelings of rivalry between helpers. A person may tell the pastor how helpful he is, not at all like the useless doctor he also sees. The pastor is tempted to feel proud, little realizing that the doctor may have been told in turn how good he is, and how unhelpful the clergyman is; or that perhaps both of them are run down when the client speaks to the social worker. The pastoral counsellor who is flattered to his face can never be sure of what is being said behind his back, particularly when other helpers are involved. Whenever possible the counsellor tries to lead the client to express both the good and the bad feelings, the positive and the negative reactions, to himself. It also helps if the client can be persuaded to rely on one person alone for counselling help, even if others have to be involved for medical or welfare purposes.

By encouraging the acknowledgement and expression of good and bad feelings towards one person—the counsellor—the defence pattern will begin to shift. The helper can also point out the splitting occurring with other significant figures, previously seen only in a one-sided way. The husband who is only described as 'bad' must have some good qualities as well, while the mother who is always described as caring and understanding may also at times be selfish and possessive.

Isolation is a similar defence, in which a particular feeling is withheld from its true object, sometimes being split off on to another. The man who can only feel sexually potent with a woman for whom he feels nothing but sexual desire, and who can only relate to his wife in a non-sexual way, is holding back and isolating his sexual feelings from his relationship with his wife—who is perhaps over-identified with his mother, for whom he must not have sexual desire. He splits off the sexual feelings with a second woman. But the defence is also seen in other ways, as in intellectualization, where an emotion is talked about, but is not felt—as if it should be there, but cannot surface in real feeling. Some people demonstrate such resistance by talking much about themselves, often analysing themselves intellectually, but showing little human feeling in their contact with the helper or with others. Frustrating though this may be for the counsellor, he can guide the client to see that he cannot acknowledge his feelings because he is afraid of being overwhelmed by them, or for fear of hurting others. Isolation of feeling can take different forms—such as joking about everything, chatting about trivial matters, talking in a generalized way, or even trying to get the counsellor to talk about himself. Here again the helper looks for reasons for such resistance: e.g. 'You seem to find it amusing—I guess it is difficult to admit other feelings you may have in case they hurt too much.' Or, 'We keep going round and round on this same point. I wonder if there is anything else which you are finding difficult to tell me, because you are afraid I won't understand.'

Denial bears some resemblance to isolation, although it is more explicit. Vehement denial is particularly obvious, and can be seen as fear of acknowledging something which is too close to the truth. 'Methinks the lady doth protest too much.' It is nonetheless presumptuous to regard every denial as indicative of the opposite feeling. This 'heads I win, tails you lose' argument typified too much of early psychoanalytic polemics. The counsellor needs to distinguish those occasions when the client's denial is genuine, therefore indicating that a remark of the counsellor's is mistaken, and defensive denial, where a person may or may not be conscious of the truth. The man who works for an ailing company which is about to go bankrupt, and who says, 'I'm not worried about losing my job,' could be denying his worry about facing unemployment, but he could equally be genuinely pleased at the prospect of early retirement from a job which has been unsatisfactory. Other clues will help to determine the probable truth behind any denial:

Mrs Osmond had taken her child to the doctor, and was

told that the child would have to see a consultant at the local hospital. 'But I'm not worried about him,' says Mrs Osmond to the health visitor. As she goes on, she mentions several people whom she knows who have been to doctors and been told that nothing is wrong, only to discover later that they have serious physical conditions. At this point the health visitor can confirm the earlier suspicion that Mrs Osmond was denying how worried she is about her child. 'I think in view of what you say about these other people, you can't help being a little worried about your son, even though it is difficult to admit it to yourself. We hope the doctor was right in saying that it is just routine, but it is bound to be difficult to stop worrying altogether when you are a mother and you care as obviously as you do about him.'

The fore-runner of denial, and of many other defences is *repression,* in which feelings, thoughts and experiences are so completely forgotten, that it is as if they had never existed. They may be feelings of which a person was briefly aware, but which were rapidly pushed away, or even impulses which were not permitted to emerge into consciousness because they were felt to be so threatening. In everyday circumstances names and details about people can be forgotten, but here the repression is partial because we know we have forgotten. Where repression is total we have even forgotten that we have forgotten. Painful or uncomfortable memories are hidden away, although repressed feelings have a way of slipping out sideways, such as in slips of the tongue, or more seriously in psychosomatic symptoms.

Psychosomatic symptoms can also result from another defence mechanism known as *introjection,* in which the physical and personal characteristics of a significant person are incorporated or identified with. Introjection is an important positive feature of grieving. Problems tend to arise when hostile feelings towards someone significant cannot be acknowledged, and some negative feature is introjected. A person who has been criticized might in turn attack the next person below him in the pecking order — taking in and taking on the role of the one who has attacked him, against whom he cannot retaliate. The child who has been to the dentist and

had a painful filling comes home and proceeds to show
aggression to a younger brother or sister; or less harmfully
displays the introjection by playing at being dentist to one of
the dolls. The patient with a pain in the chest might have had
a relative who recently died of a heart-attack, or the patient
with a headache turns out to have lost her closest friend who
died as a result of a brain tumour. These latter examples will
not be unfamiliar to the general practitioner. They are ways
of coping with grief, and in particular with negative feelings
towards the one who had died, leaving a person feeling alone
and unloved, yet unable to acknowledge his resentment.

A variation of introjection is *'turning against the self'* — seen,
for example, in masochistic tendencies which are a substitute
for the expression of sadistic or aggressive wishes towards
another. Suicide attempts may sometimes be a last desperate
attempt to cope with hostility felt towards a person who is
also loved. Because of fear of hurting the other, or fear of
losing their love, an attempt at suicide turns the anger against
the self. At the same time it can hurt others, who are then
made to feel guilty, and it has the effect (often seen by those
who survive such an attempt) of partially succeeding in
expressing hostility. Those who survive such attempts may
feel even more guilty when they see this. Turning against self
is also seen in the self-hatred of some people who are
depressed; here again, the efforts of those around them to
help often flounder against the rock of self-contempt, and
have a depressing effect on these other people as well.
Depression can therefore become a very effective way of
expressing anger, while apparently remaining innocent and
blameless of deliberate hostility.

Projection is a very commonly used defence. Feelings which
cannot be owned are attributed to another or others, and
sometimes condemned in them. Since projection is not made
at random, but often has some basis in reality, the person on
to whom the projection is made fits in some way, making
recognition and owning of the defence more difficult. A person
may find it less uncomfortable to say 'He is angry with me'
than to admit 'I am angry with him', or 'She is jealous of me'
when in fact 'I am jealous of her'. Some projections may be
attached to the pastor. If the helper's attitudes and opinions
are not obviously known (less easy to achieve in many pastoral

settings) the counsellor can more easily demonstrate that
what has been attributed to him is not based on fact, and that
such opinions really are the client's projections.

'You must dislike me after what I said last week,' says the
client. The helper first finds out whether there is any
justification for the client thinking this from anything he
said or did. 'What makes you think that? Did I appear to
show dislike for you last week?'

'Well, no, I just thought that. I would feel it if I were
you.'

'I think, then, you are projecting on to me your own
difficulties about accepting yourself, warts and all.'

Another surprisingly common remark, particularly from
hesitant clients in the early stages of counselling, is: 'I think I
must be wasting your time.' Although this may indicate a
difficulty in allowing themselves to claim attention, it can
also disguise the client's feeling that counselling is a waste of
time, because it has apparently got nowhere in the initial
meeting.

Reaction-formation is the name given to an over-reaction to
certain thoughts or emotions. If a person is afraid of
experiencing positive feelings (often because of a fear of being
let down by the object of such feelings) he may react against
them by becoming belligerent, or distant. More commonly the
over-reaction takes the form of *idealization,* where the person
idolizes another (who is often someone in a 'parental' position
like a doctor or a clergyman), regarding the other as perfect,
even like a god or goddess, unable to acknowledge the other's
imperfections, or his anger at the shortcomings of the other.
The greater the idealization the greater the hostility is
disguised. Reaction-formation is also seen in the over-angry
rebellious person who reacts against fears of conforming or
feelings of dependency. Other examples include the person
who is extreme in his cleanliness or tidiness, reacting against
the wish to make a mess. The person who campaigns
vehemently for censorship may be reacting against violent or
sexual wishes in himself. Even fear can be a reaction against
an unacknowledged wish, although it is often difficult to
make this paradox clear. More evidence will be needed to
substantiate such an observation. Nightmares illustrate the

phenomenon; dreams often express inner conflicts with the different figures or symbols representing different 'parts' of the dreamer. What is feared within the dream comes from within the dreamer, and may therefore be a symbol of a wish.

Reaction-formation is often characteristic of the obsessional person, and is sometimes taken a stage further into another defensive manoeuvre called *undoing.* It can be seen in compulsive behaviour, which is recognized by the client as being irrational, but is not easily controlled—e.g. frequent hand-washing, checking light switches, door latches, the avoidance of certain numbers, etc. Superstitions are fairly widespread, even if they are apparently taken lightly—such as throwing spilt salt over the shoulder. (Which hand, which shoulder—all the permutations are jokingly tried!) It is as if performing such rituals exerts magical influence, containing anxiety or cancelling-out guilt and the consequent threat of punishment. Ritualistic actions can be felt to be so significant that they cannot be given up. Clergy trained in the Anglo-Catholic or pre-Vatican Two traditions will be familiar with the horror and sense of dread which some devout Catholics felt when the rituals in worship were not performed exactly according to the rules. Some people felt (perhaps still feel?) that such errors were more sinful than violations of rules of personal conduct.

The defences which are seen at work in ourselves and others are legion. *Asceticism,* for instance, which has a noble tradition in the spiritual life, can also be a type of reaction-formation, more commonly seen in adolescents. There may be dramatic swings between the ardent expression of sexual feelings (in masturbation in particular with young men) and periods of abstinence and great purity. In young women asceticism more frequently takes the form of strict dieting, in its extreme form seen in anorexia nervosa. The reasons for fasting are complex, but include a reaction against the wish to eat voraciously, or against developing into a mature sexual adult.

Rationalization describes the apparently plausible reason given for a wish which is being denied. In anorexia, for example, dieting can be rationalized on the grounds of the wish to be fashionably slim and attractive, although this is accompanied by the inability to see just how thin and wasted the body has become. In the church, as in other spheres of life, rational arguments can disguise unconscious fears. At the risk of making sweeping statements, debates about the ordination of women, for instance, appear to revolve around scriptural and theological precedent, but may disguise the threat to the all-male authorities of the church of allowing women to become too 'powerful'.

Regression and fixation are defences which both relate to earlier stages of development. In the former a person can regress in the face of anxieties about the present or the next stage of life; for example the middle-aged man who plays at being an adolescent may be doing so to avoid the anxiety aroused by aging. *Fixation* describes the failure to move in certain respects beyond a particular stage of development, as in the Peter Pan character, or the playboy type who stays adolescent, or even pre-adolescent in attitude, because the next stage of life — intimacy and responsibility — is seen as too threatening. Both these defences can be more easily understood in the context of the model of human development proposed by such writers as Erik Erikson.[1] A book on practical skills is not the right place to develop the implications of the study of personal growth and maturity for pastoral and other helping work. Nevertheless, the pastor, like other helpers, should make this part of his study, especially if he wishes to engage in counselling. Some books are suggested in Appendix B, and in 'Suggestions for Further Reading'. I hope myself to develop in a later book ways of using the Erikson model in counselling and other pastoral situations, especially looking at the relationship of the stages of life to presenting problems and the counsellor-client interaction.

Finally we come to two defences which at first appear very similar. Psychodynamic writers distinguish between *displacement* as a defence mechanism which, like other defences, does not always work, and *sublimation* which strictly speaking is not a defence at all, since it presupposes successful resolution of conflict. It is a sign of healthy development. In practice successful displacement is very hard to distinguish from sublimation.

Displacement describes the redirection of feelings and impulses away from an original object on to another. Let us suppose that, instead of expressing anger with a child, father kicks the cat. As far as the cat is concerned this is not a very successful displacement; father might have done better to kick a door, or to go and play a game of football, where his aggression could be redirected in a more socially acceptable way. What is acceptable, and what is unacceptable displacement varies from culture to culture, and from social class to social class. At first sight kicking the cat might appear to be an example of displacement, whereas kicking a football is an example of sublimation. But if father was unable to express any anger to the child, kicking the football cannot be called sublimation, since it might have been appropriate at least to have told the child off, and expressed some anger. Strictly speaking, sublimation describes a stage of personal development, where feelings can be expressed directly, but to an appropriate degree, and where surplus feeling can also be directed into other socially and culturally acceptable forms. Freud believed that civilization is built upon the sublimation of basic human emotions and desires into wider activities, such as science, technology, art and literature—and, we may wish to add, into caring for others.

Sublimation is a term usually reserved for this redirected expression of feelings and desires in a mature form. A nun, for instance, enters an order which looks after orphaned children, and in doing so she inhibits her sexuality and her capacity to bear children. At the same time she is able to sublimate her maternal wishes in looking after the children in her care. Let us suppose that another nun in the same order becomes emotionally unstable, showing signs of extreme possessiveness with some of the children, and jealousy towards the other nuns. In her case sublimation is not the right description. Her wish to enter the order was a displacement of her wish to be a mother, which has since broken down. She had not sufficiently worked through the feelings involved when taking her vows. The nun who has fully recognized her feelings, and on that basis consciously chosen to inhibit them, is able to sublimate successfully, and use her feelings not only for her own fulfilment, but for that of the children in her care.

We may ask why it is necessary to make such distinctions. They seem to me to raise questions about the interpretation of moral and cultural values which we cannot avoid. That one action is felt to be reasonable, and normal, and is therefore labelled 'sublimation', while another is less acceptable psychologically and is labelled 'neurotic', 'defensive' or 'displacement' raises these questions. The standards of society, the debates of the Church, the opinions of psychologists about what constitutes mature and immature behaviour are always in a state of flux. Questions are also raised about the pastoral counsellor's own values and aims, and his model of maturity, which I shall look at again in chapter 10.

It must be stressed again that defences are necessary and natural, and that they function reasonably well nine out of ten times for nine out of ten people. Some circumstances will, however, threaten these defences, and it is these which often bring people to the helper. Some clients may want to restore the defences without looking at the underlying conflicts, and will begin to show resistance at the same time as asking for help. Resistance, as much as defences, serves a purpose, warding off anxiety about talking about certain subjects, desires, or thoughts which might lead to fear, guilt or shame. The pastoral counsellor appreciates this anxiety. He offers co-operation to help overcome the resistance. Simply to attack it head on will more probably result in a strengthening of the barriers against the counsellor, and against the conflicts within.

> This very simple example of handling resistance comes from the end of a first interview with Pat, a teenager who shed many tears over a boyfriend who had just left her. Towards the end of the time the youth club warden asked Pat whether she would like to return next week and talk further. She hesitated. 'You're not sure,' he observed. 'No, I'm not, I don't want to be silly.' Since she had earlier murmured something about being silly when she was crying, the warden went on: 'Perhaps you are not sure about coming back because you're afraid I will think you are silly if you get upset?' 'I'll come,' Pat replied promptly.

Notice here how the counsellor frames his observation, stating first the resistance (not coming back) because of the anxiety (he will think I am silly) if she allows herself to show her true feeling (crying). If the helper can gauge what the client is trying to avoid (being upset, shame, embarrassment, feeling angry, allowing the helper to get too close) he can point out the resistance and the reason for it. Observing resistance alone is often felt as an attack by the helper upon the client.

Examples of resistance include missing appointments, arriving late, and breaking off counselling altogether. Reactions like this are not necessarily resistance alone, but can be the result of incompetent counselling. A helper must not impute defences and resistance to a client without first considering whether he has himself mishandled the situation, perhaps having said or done something which caused offence. But where a counsellor is used to good relationships with most people, the exceptions who miss sessions or come late might be seen as acting out their anxiety, which they are unable to share more directly. Sometimes clients act out their disappointment when the counsellor has inadvertently let them down; e.g. where a helper has had to cancel or postpone a session, or when he takes a holiday. Such acting out becomes a kind of 'tit for tat', letting the helper down, or giving him a taste of his own medicine.

Resistance is also seen in those who reject whatever the pastor tries to say, or in others who accept submissively all that is said. Those who reject may be afraid of letting the counsellor get too near the truth, or fear that if he is right he will begin to control them. Those who meekly accept may be afraid to challenge or to disagree, or fear looking more closely at themselves. Instead they swallow what is offered whole, without pausing to digest it. Passivity can be as frustrating to the helper as outright rejection. Resistance is shown too by the client who flatters or idealizes the counsellor, or by the client who tries to seduce him through sexual talk, and by the client who tries to get the counsellor to talk about himself. These ploys, whether conscious or unconscious, act like a smokescreen to lead the helper away from the real areas of concern.

It should not be assumed that resistance is bound to intrude significantly on the counselling relationship. Many people value the opportunity to express themselves, and do so fairly fully. Many will be helped because their helper listens carefully, and reflects back accurately. With some people resistance occurs at certain points only, and when overcome leads to more openness and insight. With some, however, there is little sign of change. Instead of working through different issues, moving further all the time, the meetings appear to go round and round in circles, or there is no change whatever reported. This may mean that there is a limit to what can be achieved, or indicate that alternative approaches should be considered — medication, behaviour therapy, or psychotherapy, depending upon the particular circumstances. Some resistance may not just be to the expression of thoughts, but resistance to change itself. Again the counsellor looks for reasons why this should be so, rather than aggressively confronting the barriers.

More may be gained, for example, from 'being ill' than from being well. Distress can become a powerful way of mobilizing care, deterring anger, or seeking attention. Attention-seeking is often used pejoratively, but it disguises a genuine need. What needs to be questioned is whether being 'sick' or depressed is the only way of getting a response from others. What prevents such attention-seekers from believing they have positive qualities which will evoke esteem? Sometimes, especially where there is a contract coming to an end, a person seems to get worse, with the original difficulties returning, or with the onset of new problems. The prospect of 'going it alone' makes some people very frightened, particularly when they have come to depend upon the helper. Their new problems may be a way of saying, 'I need to go on seeing you; I can't let you go; how can you be so harsh as to stop seeing me when you can see I'm no better?' The counsellor need not deny the reality of the problems, but he does recognize that they are, albeit unconsciously, a way of resisting the end of the helping relationship.

This type of resistance to change has been called 'the gain from illness'. The opposite of this is another form of resistance to change, called 'the flight into health' — seen most dramatically when people are genuinely desperate at the first interview, but come to the second miraculously better — miraculous because there is no obvious reason either to them or to the helper to account for the change. By becoming better they may be disguising from themselves and the counsellor their worries about talking and where it is likely to lead them. Such worries are genuine. They are terrified of what they will uncover if they pause to look within. In most cases this fear is out of all proportion to what they actually find if they do go on. It can, nonetheless, be a powerful reason for resistance. Change may be difficult too if it implies a threat to existing relationships. The wife who is constantly insulted by her husband may be able to recognize what is happening, and even her own contribution to it, but feels powerless to alter her own submissive behaviour. The change may cause an even greater threat to her husband, and so perhaps to the marriage. For this reason it is desirable (though not always possible) that people should feel support from those close to them, when they seek help. If there is enough support it might be possible to see a couple together, because change in one partner often means consequent changes for the other. Where this does not happen an absent partner can be used as a rationalization for not changing. If they can be seen together such reasons can be checked or challenged. Family therapy has similar advantages, especially where children are involved in the problem. The dynamics of counselling a couple or a family, and the dynamics inherent in groupwork are more complex even than those in one-to-one counselling, and cannot be looked at here. In practice, the counselling of couples, families or in groups may only be a small proportion of pastoral work. It should not be forgotten that even individual counselling can help people effect change in those around them (see the example of Mrs Lamb, pages 75-7).

Eugene Kennedy makes a useful distinction between resistance and reluctance.[2] He uses reluctance as a more accurate description of the attitude in those who see the helper, or are seen by the helper, at someone else's insistence. They come under duress and under pressure to please a third party. Resistance is not such an appropriate term to use of those who are fully aware that they have not chosen to come, and do not wish to be there. The helper may not be able to enlist the co-operation of the reluctant person against barriers and other signs of resistance, when he has not asked for help and may be suspicious of the counsellor.

The reluctant person will prove very difficult to work with unless the pastor can create a sense of rapport and trust. This can sometimes be achieved by openly acknowledging the compulsion and threat to the client, and by talking about the way he feels about it. Analysing the resistance in any deeper way will be dismissed as irrelevant and confirm suspicions. The reluctant client is sometimes surprised by such understanding, and decides to go on seeing the pastor, but of his own free will. Alternatively he realizes that the pastor is not going to force him to come, and although he chooses not to come again then, he perhaps returns at a later date, to see him or another helper. Again this will then be his own decision, and not made simply to please or propitiate others. Working with reluctant people illustrates indeed the cardinal principles of all that has been written in this chapter:

first, accept that there is a good reason for resistance;

secondly, draw attention to the resistance itself;

thirdly, suggest or attempt to discover why there is resistance;

and finally, create a sense of trust which enables the barriers to be lowered, in order to reach the particular feelings which initially gave rise to them.

Notes

1. Erik Erikson, *Childhood and Society.* Penguin 1965, chapter 7.
2. Eugene Kennedy, *On Becoming a Counsellor.* Gill and Macmillan, Dublin, 1977, pp. 84-90.

NINE

Ways of Relating

If there is one theme which runs through this book, it is certainly the centrality of the relationship between the pastoral counsellor and each individual person, a relationship based not upon forcefulness of personality, but upon the 'still, small voice' (in words and manner) of acceptance and of gentleness, combined with a clear sense of purpose and incisiveness. Counselling, pastoral care and certain other situations differ from other 'services' inasmuch as the skills are mediated so much through the manner of the helper that without this central relationship all manner of technique will fail.

I have already observed (chapter 5) that those who deal directly with 'the public' will be felt to be better at their job when they can relate well to their 'clients'. Even the much maligned second-hand car salesman needs to create a sense of trust and respect. The ability of others, such as teachers and doctors, to project themselves positively increases the effectiveness of their professional skills. The clergyman who is well-liked will probably also have more notice taken of his sermons, or his appeals to the laity to be involved in the Christian ministry. But in all these instances, once the good relationship has been formed, it can be taken for granted, allowing the student to concentrate upon learning, the patient to follow 'doctor's orders', and the parishioner to sustain his own part in the life of the church.

In some respects the counselling relationship can also be taken for granted where it is predominantly positive. Research into the effectiveness of counsellors has confirmed the desirability of personal qualities such as warmth, empathy, sensitivity, congruence and non-possessive love.[1] However, many counselling approaches have more to say about the use of the relationship between counsellor and client. Many, for instance, encourage the counsellor to monitor the feelings evoked in him by the client and to reflect these feelings back in a sensitive manner, demonstrating how the client may appear to others. The analytic model goes even further than this, and suggests that the way the client feels about the counsellor can also act as a guide towards understanding the attitudes and perceptions the client has towards others, especially to those who are most significant to him in his present life, or earlier in childhood and adolescence. In both instances counselling experience suggests that it is often the monitoring of, and perception of, negative feelings in counsellor or client towards the other, or the distorted perceptions the client has of others, which provide as much opportunity for self-knowledge and consequent change, as positive feelings within the counselling relationship.

This relationship between the counsellor and the client is often more complicated than is suggested in some books about counselling. To study this interaction I shall look at it from four angles. In practice there will always be an overlap, and it may be difficult to isolate one aspect from another. Where the different elements which contribute to the relationship can be identified, the counsellor can help the client differentiate between appropriate and inappropriate ways of seeing others, and relating to them. These elements do not only appear either in the counselling itself, or in relationships with others discussed in counselling; but they are often more clearly seen there, and can be talked about more naturally than in many other settings.

The four aspects I will consider are:

1. The working relationship between the pastoral counsellor or other helper and the client, as people with a task to perform together, both accepting responsibility for the 'work' they are engaged in.

2. The 'real' relationship of two human beings.

3. The relationship which may develop through inappropriate responses, technically known as 'transference'.

4. The relationship as it develops from the counsellor's side in his response to the client, technically known as 'counter-transference'.

1. The Working Relationship

Counselling, far more so than that other approach which is better called 'advice-giving', will not be successful unless what has been called a 'working alliance' develops between the client and the helper. It was suggested in the last chapter that the client may wish the counsellor to join him in an alliance against 'the enemy within'. This motive alone—simply to get rid of offending problems or forces—is not in itself sufficient for anything other than superficial change, or restoration of the *status quo*. If there is to be a genuine alliance between counsellor and client both need to recognize that counselling involves working with inner fears and feelings, and that this best happens in a co-operative partnership. In chapter 7, a brief outline was given of the type of person who will benefit most from counselling which aims at such exploration and insight.

The motivation which brings a person has been frequently mentioned in previous chapters. Unless the client is ready to accept his part and his responsibility for the work involved in counselling, he and the helper will only experience frustration at the inability of the counsellor to perform miracles. One hour a week, which at most is the time given to the majority of people, is not long; a client may spend many other moments in inner reflection during the rest of the week. To gain any real benefit, people need to involve themselves, at least to some extent. in the situations they most fear, and at the same time try to observe and reflect upon their reactions. Some readily do this, and are able to use the hour to share their insight, with the counsellor becoming much more like the 'assistant' of Karen Horney's description of the relationship (see page 47).

This working alliance is fostered by the pastoral counsellor each time he explains his and the client's task, or the reasons behind his manner of helping. It is encouraged each time the counsellor leads the client to look for himself at his difficulties, and to share his thinking. It is shown in action when counsellor and client listen carefully to each other, and modify or refine the contributions the other makes. If the working relationship requires a client who can share experience and feelings, and who can think about himself, it obviously also requires a counsellor who can support a person's self-analysis, and who does not always have to be the one with the answers.

When clients too readily agree, or constantly disagree the relationship is not a working partnership, but a defensive one which probably has transference elements within it. If the counsellor cannot allow the client to be a full partner in the task, or allows the client to manipulate him, the relationship is influenced by counter-transference considerations. The aspect of the counsellor-client relationship being described here consists of a workmanlike attitude to a specific task, in which two fairly intelligent adults, respecting each other's intrinsic value as workers, meet to understand the less mature attitudes and behaviour of the client.

This is not to suggest that a working partnership must exist from the first point of contact. Although the potentiality for such a relationship must be apparent, the working alliance is built up throughout pastoral counselling, and particularly in the early sessions. The counsellor supports every sign in the client of the wish to reflect for himself. One of the aims of any helping process, which applies just as much to counselling, is to assist a person to help himself, and to learn ways of doing this which will continue long after the helper has retired from the scene. The counsellor works in the knowledge that he only has contact with a person for a short time. The external dialogue between them becomes internalized, with the 'still, small voice' of the counsellor being replaced by the 'still, small voice' in the other. People sometimes speak of holding conversations with themselves, as if they were talking with their counsellor. A successful working relationship leads to the client becoming responsible for the major part of the task, allowing the helper to withdraw to the periphery, providing incentive and encouragement through the regular contact. If this working relationship becomes internalized, the client will in future work through new crises in his own strength, with the support of good relationships made within the family and amongst friends.

This is not an unattainable ideal, although it must be said that brief counselling and pastoral work may not always allow sufficient time for this internalization to take place. Yet even in brief counselling the working relationship can be described, as it was in the answer given by one person to a friend who asked what went on in counselling. He perceptively replied, 'It's not like having crutches. It is rather that the counsellor is there while you struggle to learn how to walk. He doesn't stop you from falling, but he stays with you until you can use your feet.' This is a fine description in itself, but it is more. It illustrates a good working alliance in which that person became as insightful as his counsellor, because his description shows an understanding of what counselling is about which could equal that given by many counsellors.

2. The 'Real' Relationship

When we use the word 'real' we run up against semantic problems. What is real? What is not real? A dream can appear real while it lasts, as can an hallucination. As we look at transference and counter-transference reactions and perceptions these can be vividly 'real' to the client, or to the counsellor, although not so to another observer. The working relationship which has just been described is also real. So what do I mean by using such a word, and how does it help? It helps because we need to learn to recognize real relationships in order to distinguish possible transference and counter-transference when it occurs. Some examples may illustrate this:

A pastoral counsellor is a calm and relaxed person who remains fairly quiet in his sessions, allowing his clients to take the initiative. With most people this works well enough, although there are some who are so passive that with them he adapts his approach and becomes more active. With a few of the most passive people he even carries on a straightforward conversation.

Mr Quentin is one of his clients who has responded easily to his quiet manner. He talks freely, reflects upon what the counsellor says, and has made a good working relationship. One day he observes to the counsellor, 'You're very quiet. You don't say much, do you?' The counsellor replies, 'That's right, I do keep quiet as you've noticed, because I want to listen to what you are saying. I hadn't felt that worried you, but I wonder why you say that at this point?' In this case the counsellor is able to acknowledge that he has been seen in a real way, gives an explanation, and explores why the matter has been raised.

Mr Ingles, on the other hand, is one of those people with whom the counsellor has to intervene actively, and he speaks almost as much as Mr Ingles does. When he says, 'You're quiet, aren't you? I don't like these silences,' the counsellor is aware that this is not a real perception. It is, of course, real to Mr Ingles, who is distinctly uncomfortable. Yet it does not ring true for the counsellor. What is Mr Ingles expecting? He may be saying more about himself than about the counsellor, since he is a quiet person. Is he afraid in case there really is a silence? Is he expecting more (advice perhaps?) than the reflection back of his own words. In this case the counsellor picks up the inaccurate perception of himself, and uses it to clarify what the man is thinking. 'I wonder what leads you to say that, when I actually feel I am talking a lot? You seem to be feeling uncomfortable.'

Miss Ryan is training to be a counsellor, and is seeing a therapist over certain problems about close relationships. She tells him one day that his room is not as colourful as her supervisor's office. The therapist knows the supervisor and it is true that she has a lot of bright pictures and *objets d'art*: his own room, by contrast is quite restrained in its decoration. Miss Ryan's perception is an accurate one. However, she goes on to say that he is a very cold and distant person and that his room typifies this. The therapist feels that he actually shows warmth and humour in her sessions, because she is herself a sociable person with whom it is easy to feel relaxed. He also shares with her some of his technical thinking since he is aware that this might help her in her own training. There have been several occasions when they have shared some amusement in the sessions. Her description of his room might be accurate, but her description of him is not, and he feels that she is defending against the wish to be warm and close to him by seeing him as cold and distant. This in fact mirrors how she describes herself when it comes to intimate relationships.

If the therapist just described was told by many of his clients that he was cold and distant, he would need to re-think the image he has of himself. If he cannot see that he could be so, he may have some counter-transference difficulties. A counsellor needs to be as aware as possible of the way in which he presents himself to avoid imputing to clients fantasies which are in fact real, accurate perceptions.

Furthermore, to distinguish between what is a transference reaction and what is not, the helper has to have some understanding of what is an appropriate feeling, and what is not. For example, clients often value the helper and their sessions, and feel sad when they have to stop coming. Such sadness is an appropriate and real response, and it would be unreal if some sadness were not to be present. The counsellor who cannot assess the appropriateness of sadness may begin to interpret such feelings as indicative of problems about leaving, but he would thereby be denying the reality of human experience. If, on the other hand, a client shows intense feelings of grief, or immense anger at ending, then the pastoral counsellor can with greater justification suggest that some earlier problems about endings are distorting the present situation. In suggesting this he does not imply that such intense feelings are wrong, but that they belong more aptly to a previous experience which requires some understanding.

Similarly if two people find warmth and satisfaction in their meetings, this is part of the reality of normal relationships. If these feelings become, on either side, over strong (for instance, the counsellor constantly fantasising about a sexual relationship with the client, or the client becoming angry because the helper is not physically demonstrating his love) another situation has arisen, which requires working upon in the light of what we know about transference and counter-transference feelings.

The real relationship described here differs from the working relationship, since it embraces other aspects of human interaction, and is in a sense the natural relationship which might have existed between the two people had they met in other circumstances, and not as client and counsellor. When the pastor expresses compassion or concern at something which has gone badly wrong for the other, or joins

in the laughter when they both find something genuinely
amusing, when he expresses the sadness which he might also
feel at the end of a pastoral relationship, or when he
congratulates the person upon an achievement — when he
does any of these things he overrides the working relationship
and defers for the time being the transference implications of
such responses. The real relationship is the foundation upon
which the other aspects of counselling and pastoral work are
built. It supports the working alliance, and, to change the
metaphor, acts as a backcloth against which transference
and counter-transference projections can be more clearly seen.
It does not interfere with the working relationship, or the task
of understanding transference relationships; but without it
these other facets of the pastoral counselling interaction are
unlikely to develop or succeed.

3. The Transference Relationship

What we shall look at now is not peculiar to counselling or to
psychotherapy, although it is particularly important in the
latter. Knowledge of transference reactions and transference
relationships is an essential for the counsellor, even though
he may not openly refer to it. Indeed, all those who engage in
helping or caring work, whether professionally or in a
voluntary capacity, whether for example as clergy, teachers,
doctors, or as youth club assistants, will gain from some
understanding of this phenomenon. Such people are probably
already aware that those whom they work with can develop
distorted images of them. Anyone who is in a position of
helping others, or has some authority over them, becomes
important in more ways than is immediately obvious.

It is not extraordinary that transference reactions should
occur since they happen with such frequency in everyday life
that it would be strange if they were not to appear somewhere
in the helping relationship. Falling in love is one example of a
common transference. In the early heady days of romance the
lover endows the beloved with idealized qualities, feeling that
he or she is more than wonderful, feeling that life would be
nothing without the continual presence of the other. The
adoring and adored relationship of mother and baby is
transferred on to lover and beloved. In time reality becomes

clearer, as the lover realizes that the beloved is not ideal, that he or she has some not-so-good qualities as well as good ones, and learns that there can be partings without fear of complete loss. Another example of transference in everyday life can be seen when we react to someone because he reminds us of another, liking or disliking a person when we do not really know them. On better and fuller acquaintance we discover that our initial reaction might have been premature, and was based upon an earlier experience of another person.

Transference reactions to authority figures are far more extensive than the well-known and somewhat clichéd 'falling in love with the analyst'. There are of course those who fall in love with their priest, doctor, teacher or therapist, just as some schoolboys and girls have crushes on teachers, and some adults weave fantasy lives around film and television stars. Yet many other transference phenomena will be seen by the pastor—fear of criticism and punishment as if he were a harsh parent, being held in awe as if he were a superman with no human weaknesses, or suspicion when he tries to help because the client fears becoming dependent or losing dignity. Other examples will occur to the reader. If such distortions are not always apparent towards the helper, they will almost certainly be seen in the way a client relates to others, particularly those who are most significant to him. Transference reactions are so pervasive that there are few relationships which do not contain some element of distortion based upon past experience.

A student, Sue, used to talk to the chaplain at intervals about her difficulties in making a break from her mother, who was very possessive. One day she told him that she would have to go and see her tutor and tell her how things were going. 'If I don't tell her I know she will worry about me.'

It might seem reasonable to keep a tutor informed, although the chaplain knew from the tutor that Sue reported her progress to her far more than was necessary. Had the tutor asked to see Sue regularly, it might have been reasonable for Sue to visit her so often. But in view of the mother's propensity to worry, it was more likely that Sue was attributing to her tutor characteristics which were more applicable to her mother. Sue may have been hoping that the tutor would worry about her as her mother did.

On another occasion Sue told the chaplain, 'I was very concerned after I left you last time, in case you were worried about me.' The same transference reaction was at work. The chaplain replied, 'You seem to feel that both I and your tutor are going to worry about you like your mother does. It seems to me that you almost need to have someone worrying about you, in case you feel forgotten. Perhaps that is why you ring home so often, not just because you say that mother is a worrier, but to check that she hasn't forgotten about you?'

A transference relationship is like viewing someone through coloured glass—all that is seen is transformed and perceived incorrectly. Unlike coloured glass, transference perceptions are normally not obvious to the person who looks through them, nor are they always obvious to the person seen in this way, who feels misunderstood, but does not know why. Ways of seeing start in childhood and, uncorrected, can continue to pervade the rest of life, especially as regards significant relationships.

As an example, let us suppose that a young boy experiences his mother as harsh, critical and generally uncaring. She provides his first and crucial model of a woman, and it may be difficult for him to alter this image. He might be helped by having women teachers who treat him more positively, but let us complicate his life for him and imagine that his teacher is an old dragon who does not take kindly to children like him who tend to be withdrawn. Our unfortunate boy suffers the whiplash of her tongue, and is confirmed in his view that women are to be feared. So he enters adolescence with a distorted view, also seeing what he has learned to see. Fearing women, he bungles his attempts to relate to girls, and fastens on those occasions when he is rejected to confirm his view of them. He is blind to the more positive responses given to him. He even now begins to treat women in ways which invite critical responses from them.

Having come to manhood he decides that he needs help and goes to the local counselling centre. The person who

first sees him realizes that it would be better for him to
work with a woman, in order to challenge some of his false
assumptions. He is immediately suspicious of her, taking
all that she says as an attack upon him, so that he becomes
very defensive. He expects her to be hostile, and his
rejection of her attempts to care make her feel quite angry,
although she does not reveal this to him. It is a hard task
for her to create an atmosphere in which he can trust her,
accept what she says, and communicate openly with her.

There are two ways in which the relationship with the
counsellor could help this prejudiced young man. Firstly,
the perseverance and patience of the counsellor may win
his confidence, so that, without her having to draw attention
to it, the experience of talking to her changes his attitude to
women in general. Certainly much good counselling
succeeds because it provides a new model of relating,
which demonstrates such acceptance and care. The draw-
back to this approach is that the young man could say to
himself, 'I have learned to trust this woman, but I have no
reason to think that other women are the same as her. She
is the first woman I have felt is not against me, but how do
I know that others aren't still going to do me down?
Anyway, she only cares about me because it's her job, and
she is paid to do it.'

There may be less chance of this type of reaction if the
counsellor uses an alternative approach, and makes explicit
the parallels between his view of her and his view of his
mother, teachers and other women. When he first comes to
her she therefore observes his reaction against her, his
cowing back from her, and his thinking that all that she
says is critical; and suggests that he seems to see her as if
she were his mother, which she is not. She can go on to
show him that in his present feelings about women he also
acts on past experience without checking whether it is a
realistic picture of all women. She may even be able to
show him how he has behaved with her, as if he were
trying to provoke rejection. In other words, through drawing
attention to the significance of their present relationship,
and not as in the first approach taking it for granted, she is
able to point out the transference distortions which lie at
the root of his problems with women, including the

problems he has relating to her as a counsellor.

Using the transference, particularly when it is negative, or obstructing the counselling work, demonstrates in the present difficulties which have been created in the past. Positive transference feelings, as long as they are not counter-productive, can usually be left unobserved, since they do not normally interfere with the course of counselling—they usually enhance it. Certain feelings, however, may appear positive, but can be so intense that they prevent insight. The extreme erotic transference (which is not all that common) may seem like intense love and admiration on the surface, but it is invariably a resistance towards acknowledging hostile feelings. When a client is too willing to accept everything the counsellor says, this cannot be called positive co-operation. The helper may have to interpret such a response in transference terms:

> Tom came to see a pastoral counsellor, having the previous year seen a psychiatrist for several weeks. He explained his problems, and reeled off a list of reasons for them which he said his psychiatrist had told him. He explained, amongst other things, that his parents had always ruled his life for him, and that he had always felt they were very good to him. The psychiatrist had told him that he should feel some resentment towards them. He asked the counsellor what she thought. She replied, 'I feel that you are wanting me to be like your parents, telling you what I think; you seem to find yourself wanting someone who can give you all the answers, like them or your psychiatrist. It is much more difficult for you to believe that, given help, you can work things out for yourself.'

Such an expectation, transferred from previous relationships, would, if permitted to continue, hinder the course of counselling. But such interpretations do more than pave the way for more effective use of counselling; they also point out the influence of past patterns on present behaviour, whether with the counsellor or in relation to others. Transference interpretations, like interpretations about resistance, need to be made sensitively. No one is being criticized for having false assumptions. Yet it may also come as a surprise to some people that the counsellor refers to their own relationship. People are more used to experts talking at them, and are unaccustomed to personal references to the relationship between them.

I have already referred, in chapter 2, to the triangle of insight, in which connections can be made between the past, the present and the counselling itself. Although much counselling depends upon a combination of care, listening and accurate reflection, and the healing effects of time itself, insight is encouraged when transference interpretations focus on the 'here-and-now' of the session. Such references frequently have to be made time and again before persistent patterns of behaviour and perception begin to shift. Change begins, and patterns are altered as new ways of reacting and relating are tried out with the counsellor. They may then be translated or transferred back in a new form to everyday life. The client, for instance, learns that he can disagree with the counsellor, and does not have to remain meek and passive. Through this half-way stage he may then begin to express disagreement more openly in other outside situations, especially when he realizes that his meekness and passivity are inappropriate responses more relevant to past situations. This takes time, and one clear difference between long-term and brief work is that there is more opportunity in the former to work through such insight. What may be understood rationally early on often takes much longer to be translated into deeper change.

Since there is a constant interplay between past and present, between current life inside and outside the counselling relationship, the pastoral counsellor watches for links which he might make. As stated earlier, in counselling these links are often between two points of the triangle, although with full transference interpretations counselling approaches a style which is more typical of psychodynamic psychotherapy. The following brief examples demonstrate some of the different connections which can be made:

'I'm concerned what my boss thinks about me.'
'Perhaps you are also concerned what I think about you.'
(an outside relationship linked to one with the helper)

'I keep thinking you are trying to ridicule me.'
'That sounds as if you see me like your father used to be towards you.'
(the helper related to the past)

'I notice that you often get anxious when I suggest you are angry with me. It makes me wonder whether you find it difficult to admit that you can get angry with other people as well.'
(the helper related to outside current situations)

'Isn't the criticism you fear from your teacher when you present a piece of work like the criticism you used to get as a youngster, when you felt you could never do anything right in your parents' eyes?'
(feelings in the present related to past feelings)

'You say you feel embarrassed talking about sex to me, and that seems like the embarrassment you felt when you met that girl who excited you. And both are like what you may have felt when you were younger, when your mother insisted on telling you about her sex life. You said that was embarrassing, but perhaps it was somewhat exciting too?'
(all three points of the triangle linked together)

The helper recognizes signs of transference when statements seem inappropriate and have an 'as if' quality about them. It is 'as if' the client is confusing the counsellor or another with someone else — probably a parent or parental figure from earlier experience. Nevertheless, since the client may think that his perception is correct, and not 'as if', the pastoral counsellor must be able to show some evidence for his interpretation, if he is to demonstrate that his comment is reasonable:

Miss Unwin had said, on an earlier occasion, that her boyfriend had told her to go out and enjoy herself when she was at college. That remark made all the difference to the following interpretation. In one session she talked about her father as being restrictive on her as a teenager, saying she had to stay in most of the time to work, and only letting her go out at weekends providing he took her and fetched her home. She said that she could not go out to discos when at college because her boyfriend wouldn't like it, in case she met another man. Her college counsellor suggested that she was projecting on to her boyfriend her own anxiety about meeting someone else, and that she was seeing her boyfriend as restrictive like father—she had already told him that her boyfriend was happy for her to go out.

In this example the counsellor drew attention to the way her boyfriend was seen 'as if' he were the father. If he were able to go on from there and draw attention to any anxiety she had about coming to see him because 'boyfriend wouldn't like it', he would complete the triangle of insight. However, a counsellor takes particular care over remarks which draw attention to some of the feelings towards himself. Transference interpretations related to the counsellor often lead to a deepening of the transference, and can evoke even stronger feelings. The counsellor should only open up such feelings if he feels able to handle them, and that the client will not be too frightened of them. With over-dependent people in particular primitive (early) feelings are liable to be unleashed. Pastors and others who are not trained in the handling of transference will prefer to confine their remarks to links between past and present relationships as described about others. Although he may also refer to the less highly charged feelings in relation to himself, he will need to use references to himself with considerable caution.

This does not render useless the examples of more open use of transference given above. Given some understanding of these reactions, the pastor can sometimes spot ways in which he is being seen which are not appropriate, and use that insight to throw light on other relationships about which the person is talking. Furthermore, even if a pastor avoids direct reference to transference, the occasional parishioner may nevertheless form an intense 'transferred' attachment to him. Instead of reacting by a 'cut and run' operation, or, even more damaging, getting caught up actively in it, the pastor is advised in these cases to consult with an experienced counsellor or psychotherapist.

4. The Counter-Transference Relationship

In a complicated chapter there is a further complication about the use of the term 'counter-transference', because it is used to describe somewhat different aspects of the reaction of a counsellor to a client. It was originally used of counter-productive feelings in a counsellor towards another, transferred from past experience, in much the same way as transference occurs in the client. Such feelings can obscure the pastoral counsellor's objectivity, and might even make it difficult to work with a particular type of person.

Suppose at school you were bullied by a boy with red hair, and ever since you have found it difficult to get on with redheads, since they still make you feel threatened. A red-haired person comes to see you. As a helper you may find yourself reacting against him, because of your prejudice. Alternatively you may say to yourself that you must overcome this bias, but you may then be extra careful not to say anything which could be construed as negative (here is evidence of reaction-formation). Either way your prejudice transferred from the past makes it difficult to work freely. This is one reason why it is valuable for all helpers to have the opportunity to look at their own lives, particularly at their past relationships, if only to discover where their difficulties lie.

A slightly different example: you are a strong believer in people being independent, and for much of the time this helps your approach, because you can encourage people to take initiative for themselves, and to work at their problems. However, your strong views are based upon some of your own difficulties co-operating with others, especially when there is a threat of rivalry. You may therefore have a blind spot about the ability to be dependent, or inter-dependent, which are also qualities which are important in relating to others. This blind spot may prevent you from allowing people to become more dependent on you for a while, or it may even make it difficult for you to understand the problems of people who work in teams.

Examples of such blind spots and counter-transference in

this negative sense could be multiplied, since every person has some areas of understanding where he is less sensitive. (Perhaps we should say *more* sensitive?)

The second meaning of counter-transference, which now tends to be a more common definition, refers to feelings and reactions in the helper which are evoked by the client, and can be used more positively as a way of understanding the other person. As the pastoral counsellor listens and observes he finds himself experiencing different feelings with the different people he sees. Such feelings may mirror what these people are themselves experiencing (as suggested in chapter 5) or they may be a guide to the reactions which others have to them:

> One person makes a pastor feel extremely careful about saying anything which could possibly hurt. He feels he has to handle him with kid gloves. When this person talks about 'people always shying away from me', he begins to realize why this is so, and can use that feeling to understand more fully both the person in front of him, and also what others feel in his company.

> Another person arouses strong feelings of protectiveness in the pastor and allows him to see how she presents herself to others so that they instinctively 'mother' her. He then begins to look for reasons why she should need this reaction from others.

> Yet another person speaks about events which make the pastor feel very sad, although the person shows no sign of sadness. It is possible that he cannot allow himself to feel sad, but the pastor's own reaction may lead him to observe just how upsetting is the impact of the events described.

> Finally, a person describes an encounter which made her cry, and indeed leads to tears as she talks. The incident makes the pastor feel angry, and he wonders where that feeling comes from. Perhaps she too was furious, but unable to allow herself to feel or express that particular response.

Taking this last example, we need to understand the two meanings of counter-transference in order to determine what belongs to the pastor and what belongs to the other. The anger which he feels may be because of some difficulty of his own, and may be out of place in the situation being described. That is the first meaning of counter-transference. Alternatively, it may be that he is picking up the repressed feelings accurately, and is able to use his own 'counter-transference' as a reliable guide. In that case the last example (and that preceding it) could both be examples of accurate empathy on the part of the counsellor. Although empathy is strictly a misuse of the term 'counter-transference' it is a common misuse which is not without value. The same caution applies to empathy as applies to counter-transference. The helper needs to be sure that his empathy is accurate and not simply the result of his own past experience obscuring a true response. Therefore the helper reflects first upon his feelings to determine how appropriate they are, before drawing upon them when he reflects his feelings back. As long as he can be fairly certain that it is the other person's reaction which he is also describing, and not just his idiosyncratic view, empathy and counter-transference responses enlarge the scope of his counselling.

It is easier to share empathic responses than straight counter-transference reactions. In the last example the pastor could say, 'You might have felt very angry about that too.' It is not so straightforward to share a feeling when it is the person himself who makes the helper feel angry. If there is a high degree of rapport, it might be possible to share some of this, but in most counselling situations to say 'You are making me feel very angry' would cause the client unnecessary distress. Rather than use such a direct phrase, consider alternatives, such as 'I feel as if you are trying to make me angry with you'. This distances the anger the counsellor feels, and the more tentative approach does not commit him to an arrogant statement that his own reaction is the right one. A further way of using negative feelings evoked by others is to make observations at one remove, by relating them to reactions which others might have: for example, 'You say that you find it difficult to keep friends. You tend to be sarcastic in much that you say, so I wonder if that puts them off? If I'm right, I wonder what makes you push people away like that?' In this example the person's sarcasm had tried the patience of the pastor, but he refrained from a direct remark which could have been vindictive or appeared rejecting.

There is not the same need to express positive feelings towards clients, at least in direct ways, since they will hopefully be conveyed in the counsellor's manner. This does not prevent some people asking 'Do you like me?' Even if the pastor does like this person, a direct answer misses the point of the question. Why does a person ask? What is it about the pastor which makes this person feel he is not liked? To put back the question and encourage him to explore the issue opens up more. Even a simple reply, such as 'What makes you think I don't like you?', might provide an opportunity for him to explain what he does not like about himself.

*

Every pastoral encounter contains in differing degrees of intensity each one of these four aspects of meeting. While the distinction between them is not always as clear as may appear from this chapter, separately and together they make a positive contribution to the counselling process. They provide the basis for insight and growth and change, not only for those who seek help, but also for those who offer themselves as mediators of healing.

Notes

1. C. B. Truax and R. R. Carkhuff, *Towards Effective Counselling and Psychotherapy Training and Practice.* Aldine Press, Chicago, 1967.

TEN

Beliefs and Values

Although I have related the use of counselling skills and psychodynamic understanding of the helping process to pastoral settings (as well as to other caring situations) I have so far made little reference to religious belief and practice, or to theology and ethics. I have already stated that the basic techniques of counselling apply whatever the setting in which it takes place, although refinements and limitations are evident in specific instances. Pastoral counselling is, in its structure, virtually indistinguishable from other specialist areas. I suggested in chapter 2 that what makes it distinct, apart from its setting, is the concern for the spiritual dimension, and what are called questions of 'ultimate meaning', which have a special place in pastoral work.

It would however be arrogant to suggest that beliefs and values are relevant only to *pastoral* counselling. Clearly counselling which takes place in a religious setting, or with a person known for instance to be a practising Christian (either client or counsellor) implies that spiritual matters are probably going to be talked about. But orthodox religious people are not the only ones who have beliefs and values, and I would contend that some system of belief, and certain definite values, must be present in every counsellor, whether they be 'religious' or 'humanist'.

We have also seen that those who come for help to a person who is known to represent a spiritual outlook will expect beliefs and values to be significant to the helper. This may have a counter-productive effect, with the client either wishing for, or fearing, pronouncements upon matters of doctrine and morals—such after all is a very common image of the church and of Christians, as being ready to pounce upon 'sin' and condemn it. Some religions set great store by orthodoxy and adherence to credal definitions and ethical statements. Yet it is not the 'fault' of religion alone which can lead to such views. Many people like to have an authority to slavishly follow or to kick against, and will use religion as either a mother-substitute or an Aunt Sally. However much the churches change their image, there will always be people who expect them to be different, who need the image either of a benevolent guiding parent, or the wicked despotic tyrant.

Again, such problems are not peculiar to pastoral counselling. Other counsellors have to work with clients who make false assumptions, or who hold distorted views of the counsellor's values. They sometimes expect them to be harsh and judgmental in the face of the less savoury side of life, or even amoral and radical in their moral (particularly their sexual) values. Likewise all counsellors, whether in pastoral or other settings, find themselves working with clients whose values can be diametrically opposed to their own. The pastoral counsellor will see atheists and agnostics, and the secular counsellor will see people who appear to live by faith alone. The left-wing social worker will have to work with clients who hold right-wing views, while conservative helpers will find themselves confronted by more radical clients. The Jew will work with the Christian, white people with black. All those who work in the helping professions face the problem of evaluating how much their own values, education, social background and cultural bias may help or hinder their work and their understanding of others.

I imagine that it might be possible to construct a common core of values to which most helpers would subscribe, whether they work in pastoral settings or not. Such a code would probably be so general that it would have little practical value, although it is difficult to imagine, for instance, that any counsellor could allow talk of murder to be voiced by a client without wishing to take it up. He would hope that by taking the wish seriously (though not condoning it) and trying to understand the full force of feeling, he could render it less harmful. But unusual though such a seriously meant expression of feeling might be, how would a counsellor react to a person from abroad who wishes to return home and take up arms in the struggle against a totalitarian regime? I imagine that there would be much less agreement amongst helpers on the legitimate use of violence. I suggest that just as moral theologians debate the ethical dilemmas which are posed by different issues, counsellors too, whether religious or not, have to struggle in themselves with similar issues before they are in a position to help their clients do so. Listening is no soft option. Responsibility is as much the counsellor's as the client's.

Or take another more common problem. It might be taken as axiomatic by theologians and by those who help others, that to inflict hurt and damage is no solution to life's difficulties, especially if it is done gratuitously. But there are problems about how much harm or damage is justified both in the interests of society and the family, or the individual. Simply to survive, it is sometimes necessary to say or do things which either appear to hurt, or actually cause some harm to others.

For example, a woman tells her parish priest that she has had an affair with another man, and that she does not wish to tell her husband, in case she hurts him. That may seem reasonable. However, her husband apparently ignores her and takes her for granted, and yet is immensely jealous of other men and forbids his wife to go alone to functions where she might talk to other men. Perhaps by telling him, and hurting him, she will make him think twice about what he is doing to her. This again may appear reasonable. But she could tell her husband what she feels about his attitude without having to mention the affair. Or if she believes that a good relationship can never exist between them until they can be open and honest with each other, perhaps she should tell him.

Tortuous decisions like these are not unusual. There are no simple answers when we come to questions of right and wrong. It is confusing enough to think about ethical dilemmas in the abstract, but when faced with them in the flesh we begin to realize just how many facets are involved. Some issues are clear cut, and the pastoral counsellor tries to help a person to see, through reaching his own decision, the reasonableness or unreasonableness of certain actions, although this does not mean forcing one's own beliefs upon the other. For example:

A man says in passing that he periodically gets punch

drunk and beats his wife, but the only problem he wants to talk about is his compulsive gambling. Because the counsellor believes that it is not right to beat others, and not healthy to drink so much that he loses control, he refuses to ignore these aspects. He makes every effort to get them talked about, as much as the gambling. If the client refuses he works at the barriers to this. He is clear that here are issues which cannot be avoided. He believes this, of course, not just because they are morally wrong, but because such behaviour indicates something that is psychologically wrong in the man's personality, and in his relationship with his wife. Psychology and morality often go hand in hand. The counsellor does not preach at the man, or moralize, but works towards helping the client recognize the gravity of his difficulties, so that he can learn to control his gambling and his drinking, and make a better relationship at home.

There are other issues about which the helper will have his own convictions but where he recognizes that his own values are not necessarily the right ones. He will in these instances be concerned that the client makes as clear a decision as possible, even though it may be different from his own if he were in the same predicament. For example:

A woman comes to see her priest because she is pregnant and does not want the baby. She firmly believes that abortion is wrong. The parish priest does not take so straightforward a view, and in fact thinks that this is a case where, if he were asked to make a decision, he would recommend it. Of course he does not say this, because he respects the woman's right to make her own choice. He does not feel that abortion is a 'must', and so does not feel the need to persevere in questioning her objections to that solution. Instead he works with her to help her make her decision within the limits set by her own convictions.

There will be other issues where the pastoral counsellor has not clarified his own values, or where clarity is impossible. He recognizes that each situation throws up unique concerns. He may share in the confusion, though he will still wish to help the client make choices which are as thoroughly thought out as possible. For example:

> A man comes to see a pastoral counsellor about depression. He says that he is a homosexual living with a partner, and that he is convinced that his homosexuality is right. The problems seem rather to be caused by the partnership itself. The pastoral counsellor may not be sure what he thinks about homosexuality: is it so immutable in an adult that it must be accepted that some people naturally have that sexual orientation? Or is it the result of environmental factors which can be worked through in counselling, enabling a person who so wishes to become heterosexual? The pastor in this case is prepared to accept what the client says, that the homosexuality itself is no problem, but reserves his judgment on the issue. Should there be signs that this client is holding back anxieties about his sexuality, he is ready to move with him to help him work on these complex and confusing issues.

The pastoral counsellor, particularly if more at home with moral theology than with psychodynamic theory, may need to make a substantial shift in his thinking when faced with some problems. It is tempting to become hooked on moral questions when the issues at stake are in fact psychodynamic ones. The following example is a case in point:

> Vince was explaining to his minister that he and his wife were having difficulties. His wife was subject to a lot of abuse from some loud-mouthed adolescents who lived in their street; every time she went in and out of the house they would taunt her, and she had become very depressed. Vince explained that he found it difficult to tell the boys off, and he felt very weak since he could not protect his wife. It then emerged that one of his friends had come round the day before, witnessed the taunting, and had really torn the boys off a strip. This had filled Vince's wife with admiration. Some weeks later Vince told the minister that she had told him that she had fallen for his friend, and wanted to sleep with him. The friend wanted this too.
>
> When Vince first mentioned this he was obviously in a dilemma. Should he let his friend and his wife sleep

together? After all, it was what a lot of people were doing these days, and if his wife wanted to it was not up to him to stand in her way. She had to make her own choices about such matters.

It would have been easy for the minister to get caught up in the moral question, either telling Vince that marriage meant something more than this modern interpretation, or even, if he really felt it, saying that as long as there was love in the relationship, and no one was hurt, that Vince's attitude seemed very generous. Husbands cannot tell their wives what to do, as if they own them.

Either way he would have missed an important issue, which is not a purely moral one. In fact the minister asked Vince what he himself felt, forgetting for the time being what his wife and friend felt about the suggestion. Vince promptly replied that he did not want her sleeping with his friend at all. 'And it's difficult to be firm enough to say that to her. You have your opinion too, which she doesn't have to take notice of, but you are afraid to tell her what you want?' The minister felt that it was quite possible that Vince's wife was probably testing her husband to see if he was as assertive and as manly as his friend. When Vince began to push himself more, at home as well as outside, there was a lot of turmoil around as others had to adjust to this new situation—his wife had to adapt to his new 'image' and he lost his best friend—but the marriage in the end became much richer, and there was much more equality in their decision-making.

Whatever the issue, and whatever the views of the pastoral counsellor, certain principles apply within counselling which do not necessarily apply to other pastoral situations, for example when a pastor is asked an opinion in a discussion group, or when he is preaching or teaching.

Firstly, where the helper holds a particular belief or ethical view which is completely at variance with the client's, and which the counsellor feels will threaten their working relationship, he should declare his interest: for example, 'You have said that you feel very antagonistic towards religion, yet I believe strongly in the Christian faith. I shall not force my views upon you, and your own views will not offend me, but I think you should know where I stand as much as I know your own position.' Or, 'I don't believe in abortion, and for that reason I don't think I am the best person you can talk to, unless you feel that my conviction is not going to affect the help I can offer you, and won't unduly influence your ultimate decision.'

Secondly, beliefs should not be forced, whether by giving authoritative or authoritarian advice, by teaching, or even by manipulation—which is why interests may have to be declared. It is impossible to avoid manipulation completely, especially since conscious manipulation forced underground may emerge in less subtle ways. Every counsellor, for instance, tends to encourage what he believes is positive, and to explore what he feels is negative—though what he sees as positive or negative behaviour or attitudes is part of his own belief system. As far as possible the pastoral counsellor needs to be aware that his own views may impose limitations on the help he can offer.

Thirdly, counselling aims to help a person make his own choices, and this will be better achieved by enabling him to think through the different answers which follow given questions. The counsellor will sometimes act as 'devil's advocate,' however much he feels that some answers suggested by the person are potentially right. He does this because he is concerned not only with the solutions themselves, but with the underlying motivation for them:

> A parishioner starts coming to church and talks of her belief in the Christian gospel, despite her saying only a few weeks before that she was a life-long agnostic. Is this new conviction on her part genuine, or is it an (unconscious) wish to identify with the pastor, and curry his favour, because she knows the church is important to him? By acting the devil's advocate the pastor may help her take a closer look at her change of heart, even though in other circumstances he would have seen this change on her part as a very positive step forward.

Finally, the pastoral counsellor must respect the choices made by the other. He should not try to alter them when it is clear that no further talking or interpretation is likely to change a decision. This does not mean that he has to agree

with every decision, and he may sometimes say so, especially
when he feels that decisions could lead to damaging
consequences either for the person or for others:

'If you are determined to break the law, that must be your
choice. You know, of course, that you are subject to the
law, and that if you're caught you are likely to be punished.
I wonder if we could think about that, whether you are
wanting to kick against authority?'

'I think you would be unwise to leave your husband at this
time because we are still considering how the relationship
is going wrong and looking to see if there are ways of
making it a better one. But if you have to make that choice
now, obviously you will go ahead with it.'

'I can't stop you from cheating others, but if you are
determined to go on doing so, and telling me about it
beforehand, you are making it difficult for me to go on
seeing you, since you are putting me in an impossible
position with regard to others for whom I am also
responsible.'

'You are free to refuse to see a doctor if you feel you must,
but I think you need some extra help from him as well as
any help I can give you. I cannot offer you counselling
unless you get some help from the doctor as well.'

Such situations are, of course, rare, although every counsellor
must be prepared for such issues, in order not to fudge them
when they occur. There will be times with some people when
persuasion or talking fails, and when it becomes necessary to
be firm and decisive. As I have indicated previously, caring is
not synonymous with 'being soft' and accepting is not the
same as condoning.

One particular area which will obviously be central for
pastoral counsellors concerns questions of religious belief.
The chapter on barriers and the section on transference
looked at the distorted pictures which people may have of
themselves and of others. Religion can also be used
defensively, and perhaps there is no better object for
transference projections than God, who by definition is
(amongst other things) 'invisible' and 'unknowable', making

it difficult to distinguish 'reality' from transference when there is God-talk.

Since this book is concerned with practical matters, there are other works which are better referred to for the relationship between theology and psychodynamic theory.[1] A short study of such matters, from the psychoanalytic side, which balances Freud's criticism, is Erich Fromm's *Psychoanalysis and Religion.* He overturns Freud's dictum that religion is a collective neurosis of mankind, suggesting instead that neurosis is a private form of religion.[2] 'Anyone who fails to achieve maturity and integration develops a neurosis of one kind or another.'[3] He draws the type of distinction we have looked at in the practice of pastoral counselling between authoritarian and humanistic religion; in the former (which is not confined to religion as such, but is also seen in secular belief systems such as fascism or some forms of communism) the life of the individual becomes insignificant. Man's worth and strength is denied. Authoritarian religion is based upon the desire for power, or upon a leader to whom personal conscience is sacrificed (as indeed Freud pointed out in his study of the church in *Group Psychology*[4]). Humanistic religion, on the other hand, is centred around man and his strength, promoting the power of individual reason, and assisting man to recognize his limitations as well as his capabilities. It encourages principles and norms to guide men in developing their powers of love for themselves and for all living things. Faith is conviction based upon one's own thought and feeling, and not on obedience to the dictates of others. The mark of humanistic religion is 'joy', while that of authoritarian religion is 'sorrow' and 'guilt'.

By humanistic religion Fromm does not mean humanism. 'Inasmuch as humanistic religions are theistic, God is a symbol of *man's own powers* which he tries to realize in his life, and is not a symbol of force and domination, having *power over man.*'[5]

Pastoral counsellors—and indeed others who counsel those with religious conviction—will find some who use religion defensively, as a means of warding off unacceptable thoughts and feelings. God, the Bible, or the church has told them that they must suppress sexual feelings, that they must not masturbate, that they must not have sex outside marriage, and that they must not even have sexual thoughts. Others suggest that Christians are not permitted to show, or even feel, anger, and must accept any opprobrium which is heaped upon them by others as sent by God. Some fear the punishment of God, while others deny that they have any anxiety about death, because they must have unshakeable belief in the resurrection. Some project their own 'badness' on to the devil or on to some external evil force, while others even ascribe all their 'goodness' to God, unable to own either the good or the bad within themselves. Religious people are not alone in doing this, since those who have no religious faith can equally refuse to recognize their part in bad situations, or deny their own value. Some religious people use rituals and prayers as a way of suppressing 'evil' thoughts, or feel sinful and guilty if they have not performed their religious practices assiduously.

This catalogue of religious vices is perhaps contentious. Some people who have particularly deeply held religious views on some matters will dispute some of these opinions. The churches are themselves divided upon such matters, with sincere Christians of different persuasions disagreeing whether sexual and angry feelings are or are not acceptable in the Christian's life. They differ about the place and value of ritual, though all perhaps agree that religious behaviour can easily become an empty cipher, whether it is catholic or evangelical, traditional or radical in its origin. Most mature Christians, including those who have written with authority upon spirituality, agree that, however strong faith is, there are always times of questioning and doubt, and that those who have unshakeable convictions are probably defensive about their faith. Questions about religious behaviour and belief are complicated by the distinction made in chapter 8 between displacement and sublimation. What is mature faith for one person, may be defensive for another.

Similar problems arise with God-talk, which can be influenced by distortions which result from transference and projection. Ideas about God frequently tell the pastor more about the thinker than about God himself, just as it was said of the theologians involved in the nineteenth-century quest for the historical Jesus that their portraits tell us more about them than about Jesus. Since the pastoral counsellor cannot

claim any better objective knowledge of God than his clients
can, he needs to listen carefully to the ideas about God which
are aired, and in particular to any parallels or contrasts
between such descriptions and the client's experience of his
parents and other significant persons. Views about God
which tie in with the client's problems can sometimes be used
to demonstrate to him how some of his perceptions are
unreal, both of his religious faith, and of other people. A clear
example of these parallels concludes this chapter, and
demonstrates how different is the approach of the pastor *qua*
counsellor to that of the pastor *qua* mediator of the faith.

Since the pastoral counsellor is also constantly developing
and refining his own ideas and beliefs, especially his models
of God and man, he will be involved in these theological
issues, which are as complex and as difficult to handle as the
moral issues raised earlier. At least moral questions are
concerned with visible problems, whereas religious belief
attempts to construct an overview. By its very nature, it will
often be concerned with unverifiable ideas and statements.
The pastor should be aware, in his work as a counsellor, that
he is not concerned with religious questions alone. If he finds
himself *only* discussing religious ideas, then either the client
or himself is probably employing an intellectual defence.
Religious thinking must be rooted in human experience, and
it is in that context alone that religious thought and feeling
will be understood. Theology is not a gloss put upon the
content of pastoral counselling—it is implicit in the counselling itself. In wrestling with human problems, conflicts and
tensions, implicit theology is made explicit, becoming truly
incarnational, even if not always expressed in traditional
theological language.

One problem which arises with some Christians (though it
is not confined to them) is the relationship between thought,
word and deed. The words in the Sermon on the Mount seem
to suggest that anger felt or verbally expressed is tantamount
to murder, and that looking sexually upon a woman is as
good as (or as bad as) committing adultery. These words
have lodged deep in the consciousness of some people. It is
seen in a similar form in the fear which others of no religious
persuasion have, of the power of fantasy, as if to imagine is
the same as to act. The words of Jesus were probably intended

in a different sense, that those who think they are holy just because they have *done* nothing wrong are no different from others, since their thoughts and words reveal that they have the same basic human emotions. He surely did not intend to support the common fear of the child that fantasy and thought alone can cause damage to others? Nevertheless, some people believe that thinking badly of another will hurt that person. The pastor may need to help a person to realize that thinking is not the same as speaking, that speaking to a counsellor particularly about negative thoughts will not damage the person spoken about, and that even speaking to anyone is not the same as physically assaulting or hurting them. Such explanations may help unacceptable thoughts and feelings to be verbalized with the consequent realization that they are often rendered less fearful and harmful. There is more danger in repressing or suppressing thoughts than in expressing them to someone who is not shocked and who can help interpret their significance. So a person may be able to express negative feelings with sufficient force to the pastoral counsellor that he can then express himself more assertively with others, without fear of a dramatic explosion. People tend to express themselves impulsively and harmfully only when they bottle up thoughts and feelings for so long that the slightest trigger sets them off. No wonder they then associate expression of sexuality or anger with disaster.

There will be some people who are seen by the pastoral counsellor who do not profess orthodox religious beliefs, but who nonetheless voice hopes, aspirations, questions and doubts, which show that they are also searching for understanding of themselves and life. They may not use Christian language or theological terms, either because they have not learned them, or because they are associated with a religious upbringing which has been unhelpful or even damaging. As in all his contacts with others, the pastoral counsellor avoids using any other language than the client's own, but he will be alive to the potentiality of such lines of exploration. He may even point out to the client that religious thinking itself is much less rigid than he assumes, that others ask the same questions, and express the same doubts. Yet as a counsellor, the pastor is not in the business of recruiting members for his own church or faith, and he should try to

avoid being limited to any one particular theological framework or language. Be the client Christian, Jew or humanist, it
is the issues perceived by him which are important. Counselling in itself does not actively promote subscription to a
particular creed or faith.

The concluding example is a good description of pastoral
counselling, which not only illustrates points of technique,
but also shows the use of defences and transferences
described earlier. Its relevance here is that it shows how
religious and psychodynamic ideas are interwoven. It is
unlikely that the course of counselling would have been the
same had this counsellor been working in a secular setting:

> A thirty-two year old married man came for pastoral
> counselling because he was often depressed, and because
> he had recurring fantasies involving young boys and girls.
> He was frightened of these fantasies, though he had no
> history of actually molesting children. He was a capable
> man in his profession, but had turned down an opportunity
> for promotion because he felt unable to handle the extra
> responsibility. At home he appeared to be, at least on the
> surface, a model husband and father. In fact he was very
> passive when it came to handling family finances, the
> discipline of his children, and the initiation of sexual
> intercourse with his wife.
>
> His family history was elicited in the first session. His
> father had been an alcoholic who had died when the son
> was eighteen. Yet he had had a good job and had only
> drunk at home in the evenings and at the weekends, until
> he fell asleep; this meant his relationship with his son was
> always distant. His mother was involved in the church,
> which the son had attended with her twice a Sunday.
> Every night mother and son had knelt at his bedside, and
> she had prayed. Her prayers consisted mainly of instruc-
> tions to God, as to how she wanted her son to behave and
> not turn out like his father. His mother had handled father's
> pay cheque and made many of the decisions. She was
> capable, and resented men being intrusive, while his father
> was passive and dependent. The client's wife had begun to
> complain about his own passivity in sex and in the
> discipline of the children.

At the end of the first session the man asked the pastoral counsellor to pray for him. The counsellor replied, 'It doesn't seem appropriate for me to pray for you right now. Let's forego prayer for a while until we understand more clearly just what's wrong.' His client reacted with surprise, silence, and then anger. He said the counsellor was not a real minister, otherwise he would not have refused a request to pray for him. He agreed to return for another session, on the understanding that prayer would be discussed.

The following sessions were very difficult, centred around the counsellor's refusal to offer prayer for his client. It emerged that the client was not a man who prayed himself, and who switched off when prayers were offered in church. Over the course of a year he developed insight into his expectation that his counsellor would take mother's place, and pray for him in order to solve the problems. He was able to tolerate his anger which arose when his passive-dependent needs were not met. He began to see how his wish to be taken care of through prayer was a feature of other aspects of his life—wanting his wife to take responsibility for sex and the children, and refusing promotion because he wanted to avoid having to shoulder responsibility and possible blame.

With this insight he began to pray himself, and reflected on the content of his prayers. He saw a conflict between wanting his problems to go away or be solved by someone else, and a desire to discover how to solve his own difficulties. Thus he was able to see a relationship between his attitude to prayer and the transference of his relationship with his mother on to his counsellor. As he desired to pray for himself the transference also changed.

After a few weeks of being on top of the world and learning to pray on his own, his new-found freedom began to crumble. His desire to pray was swiftly followed by a refusal to do so, because God did not listen anyway. He even wondered if God existed at all. The pastoral counsellor now suggested that there was possibly a link between these difficulties and his feelings towards his passive and distant alcoholic father. Father had not listened to his son's need for help in growing up, because he was lost in his alcoholic sleep. As this relationship was discussed the anger towards the father emerged. He refused to pray or even discuss prayer in the counselling.

As he accepted and mastered his anger, he became aware of great sadness too, remembering a few times when father talked to him about his own childhood. He had felt close to his father then, feeling how kind and gentle he could be. As the sadness came through, he began to pray again, feeling the sadness in his prayers, and feeling that he really understood the cry from the cross, 'My God, my God, why hast thou forsaken me?' He felt God was with him in his sadness, and began to listen to the prayers in church. His fantasies about children subsided, and he showed greater fatherly concern for the activities and welfare of his children. His continued membership of the church provided him with a way to grow further as a maturing 'man of faith', after the counselling had finished.[6]

This case is full of examples of the issues that have been raised in this and previous chapters. With the working through of the two transference distortions which emerged in the counselling, this man's religious life became a way of finding real strength and maturity, rather than continuing, as it had done in the past, the struggle with parental figures inside himself, later projected on to the counsellor and on to God. It dramatically illustrates that over a period of time pastoral counselling was able to lead beyond the presenting conflicts to a faith which was both realistic and mature.

Notes

1. See, for instance:
H. Faber, *Psychology of Religion*. SCM Press 1976. P. Homans (ed.), *The Dialogue Between Theology and Psychology*. University of Chicago Press 1968. P. Homans, *Theology After Freud*. Bobbs-Merrill, Indianapolis, 1970. R. S. Lee, *Freud and Christianity*. Penguin Books 1967.
2. E. Fromm, *Psychoanalysis and Religion*. Yale University Press 1950, p. 27.
3. Ibid., p. 28.
4. S. Freud, *Group Psychology and the Analysis of the Ego*, rev. edn. Hogarth Press, 1959.
5. E. Fromm, op. cit., p. 37 (Fromm's italics).
6. The example given, abbreviated here, appears more fully in 'Transference and Religious Practices' by James O'Laughrun, *Journal of Pastoral Care* (USA), 1979, pp. 185-9.

ELEVEN

Endings

Eschatology has always been a vital part of Christian and other religious thinking. The urgency of the 'end of days' in the New Testament acts as a spur to present faith and activity. The certainty of death—the only certainty in life—gives rise to that sense of finitude (whatever one's attitude to life after death) which has been recognized as philosophically and psychologically significant in the writing of existentialist theologians. As Macquarrie writes in his *Principles of Christian Theology:* 'Death becomes the eschaton, and as such it brings into existence a responsibility and seriousness that it could scarcely have otherwise. Death, in one sense destructive, is in another sense creative of unified, responsible selfhood, the concerns of which become ordered in the face of the end.'[1] He recognizes that this does not necessarily prevent a denial of death and finitude, jumping from one immediate concern to the next, in a quest for illusory security.

But to concentrate simply on the future end, and upon death as a natural consequence of life, is to obscure the significance of a whole series of 'deaths', some major and some minor, which take place throughout life. Growing and living involves frequent changes, separations, new beginnings, and by implication endings. Facing ultimate death is perhaps less daunting to the person who has come to terms with the many little deaths which precede it.

The pastor and the pastoral counsellor have many opportunities presented to them to be alongside people going through times of change, adjusting to separations, and facing endings. Other books in this series will look at particular times in life when the pastor can be involved in the emotional and spiritual consequences of change. Here I wish to conclude by relating such endings to the actual practice of pastoral counselling.

Consider this theme of separation, ends and new beginnings which runs through every person's life, including some
events which also relate to a significant minority. First there
is the separation from mother at birth, a literal cutting off
from the sheltered life in the womb to face the harshness of
the external world, where for the first time the baby has to
make demands to be fed and nurtured. No sooner is the
adjustment made when a further separation takes place from
breast or bottle, and a series of changes occur as the baby
moves, partly driven by natural muscular development, away
from all enveloping parental care towards coping with its
own bodily needs and functions. The wish for autonomy
encourages the child to move away from the parents for short
periods, walking away, running back again, but uncertain as
yet of allowing too great a distance. Other separations occur
outside the child's control. At any point from a year old
younger siblings may arrive on the scene and take away
mother's undivided attention, and whether there are more
children or not it dawns on the baby that other people,
especially father, have claims on mother's time. Mother may
have to go into hospital when another baby is born, or
because she is ill. Perhaps the baby or child has to spend
some time in hospital. At any time the child may have to face
more permanent separation should one of the parents be
killed, die, or leave home if a marriage breaks up.

Even if the family remains intact during infancy and
adolescence other changes take place each requiring adjustment, and for some children giving rise to considerable
distress. The child may go from home to child-minder, or
nursery group, from playgroup to school, with changes from
school to school which can happen more frequently in a
highly mobile society where new jobs often mean new homes,
and having to make new friends. As the child moves into the
teenage years the adolescent again takes some of his own
initiative for change, although the separations are not any the
less difficult—changes from school to work (or no work),
from parental rules and standards towards the development
of his own, from friendships in groups to closer companion-
ship, from friends of the same sex to those of the opposite
sex. Some young people will leave home at this time (if not
before to borstals or boarding schools). Separations continue

throughout life from friends, homes, places of work, or because others move away. If it has not already happened, the young person comes up against death more personally when grandparents, parents or even peers are lost.

And with the life cycle beginning again, though this time as parents, separations occur when babies intrude upon the intimacy of husband and wife; and as the children grow the whole series of changes and breaks are experienced from another perspective, this time as 'the older generation'. Redundancy and retirement may also give rise to stress, and, of course, the older one becomes the more consciousness there is of death itself.

Since the work of the pastoral counsellor includes integrating these past experiences into present experience, he cannot avoid coming up against one or more of these significant separations, 'deaths' and endings. Since counselling also involves breaks in various forms, it provides in itself—in addition to current problems of separation and endings—a concrete opportunity to re-experience, in the present, feelings from the past which may still be painfully active. The counsellor will be able to observe reactions to the present, including towards himself, which throw light upon past experiences. This is a good reason for the person who offers help or counselling to spell out clearly the endings which are sure to arise in the course of counselling—the end of each appointment, breaks that have to take place because of holidays and other commitments, as well as the final break when pastoral counselling has to cease, or the specific pastoral contact is due to end. He does not do this simply to be polite, but because he wishes to draw attention to endings in order to allow the feelings evoked to be brought into the open.

Since pastoral counselling or a series of pastoral visits are fairly short in duration, some people will not become too reliant upon the opportunity to talk things out, and so will not experience any great distress when it has to end. Others will have had problems which are relatively straightforwardly resolved, and for whom the cessation of regular contact is seen as a natural end. Some people, however, may have to stop seeing the pastoral counsellor prematurely, with unfinished business which they would like to pursue. Some others may see the pastor for a long time, and any ending is bound to be accompanied by some sense of loss. The more important the helper is to a person, the greater the feelings evoked by separation. There will also always be some who, however brief the contact, react even to its brevity with feelings of being let down.

Some of the reactions to endings will be 'normal', and the pastoral counsellor encourages these to be expressed as much as the apparently inappropriate reactions, which appear exaggerated. In one sense over-reaction is inappropriate, but we understand, through appreciation of transference phenomena, that they were more appropriate in relation to an earlier separation. The helper therefore does not dismiss such feelings, because they allow him and his client an opportunity to work upon the feelings carried over from the past, as well as a chance to make the present ending more acceptable.

Since a pastor becomes involved with many people in the course of his work, he can forget how important he becomes to some of those whom he sees. When he stops seeing one person there is always another to take his place. The client, however, particularly when the help given has been effective and valued, will not so easily forget the one who has helped him. For some people the pastoral counsellor will be the most important person at that stage of their lives. He will certainly continue to occupy a unique position. If the pastor has a blind spot about endings he may deny how important people are to him, and he to them; or he may have a different problem, that of being able to let people go. He is perhaps afraid that people cannot cope on their own, especially when they tell him so. He feels the need to protect them from future pain and mistakes, failing to recognize his own needs to be valued and wanted. If as a counsellor he has few clients, he may be tempted to hang on to them, giving too much time in a session, or extending counselling beyond the point when it is still necessary.

I have suggested that extreme reactions are often connected to unresolved early experiences of separation. But before describing these and other responses to the end, I wish to suggest two responses which are not normally mentioned in books on technique. Perhaps in some psychotherapy, where clients are often carefully selected and well-motivated, these two are less common. In pastoral counselling and pastoral work, where the motivation is much more varied, the relationship is usually less intense than in psychotherapy, and these responses more regularly appear.

The first is *denial*. The helper feels that there should be some response to a break, or to an ending, and suggests this to his client, only to be met with surprise and incredulity. I do not believe that this is always defensive, although in the following example it clearly was, as later events proved:

> When I first began to teach the practice of counselling, I used to give this example of denial. Wendy by all accounts should have shown some reaction to the breaks in the counselling, because she showed considerable distress when talking about past separations, and even the present absences from her family. Yet she constantly denied any feelings about the breaks from me. At the end of each term over the last three meetings I would take up references to the separations from home and others which she always talked about, and I would link them to the impending holiday and not coming to see me. After several such ends of term Wendy retorted on one occasion, 'I don't know why you keep going on about that — it's not at all relevant.' That puts me firmly in my place.
>
> There is now a sequel to the story which I can add. Having received so strong a rebuke I gave up trying to make the link until, to my surprise, in her penultimate term, she told me she had just been to her last choir practice and had suddenly realized that she was not going to be at university for much longer. She felt very sad at the thought. I reminded her that leaving would also mean leaving me. She agreed that this would be difficult too. It took a major break to help her acknowledge that there were indeed feelings about ending counselling.

The second response not normally written about is *relief*, feeling that the end of counselling is in some respects welcome. If the uncovering of self has been painful and uncomfortable, despite the helper's efforts to ease the discomfort; or if the client is frightened of becoming too dependent; or where the client comes under pressure from others — relief at ending is an understandable response. The helper may be taken by surprise, as was the pastoral counsellor who said at the end of a session which had been very distressing for the client: 'That's a difficult point at which to have to finish today.' The client visibly brightened, and replied, 'That's all right . . . I'm quite relieved that I don't have to go further into that at the moment.'

The other feelings evoked by the end vary in their intensity. When not too intense they are such as we would expect at the end of a good relationship. When more extreme they cease to be part of a natural mourning process, and demonstrate in their intensity that other dimensions are present. Common responses at endings are:

Disappointment: This shows that a person has valued pastoral counselling, and wishes it could continue, but at the same time recognizes the limits that have to be set.

Anger: This term covers a range of feelings from mild annoyance to raging fury, expressed either openly or obliquely. Anger about ending will be felt for different reasons: some people are annoyed that they have to finish just as they felt they were getting somewhere; while others are annoyed because in leaving they feel they have got nowhere at all; some express anger when they feel they are being let down by suggesting that the help given has failed — they have to run down (sometimes only temporarily) its value, because they will not then miss something which they have decided was no good; others feel angry at having to stop at a crucial point in their self-discovery; and some feel that the counsellor does not care because his limits are seen as a refusal and a rejection. Sometimes the anger is expressed in tears; sometimes intense grief is expressed by being openly hostile. Since anger and tears are two sides of the same grieving process, the counsellor who is presented with one side should look for opportunities to draw out the other.

Sadness: This may well be felt (rather than more extreme grief) when people have found counselling valuable, and when the relationship with the pastoral counsellor has meant a lot to them. Indeed we might say that at the end of any ongoing pastoral contact, after feelings of disappointment and anger have been voiced, sadness is to be expected. Where the ending comes at the right point, this sadness is mingled with hope for the future. One writer describes a client who left the last session with tears in his eyes but a smile on his face.[2] Similarly, the pastoral counsellor who has valued the client and shares his sense of achievement will feel the sadness involved in letting go.

Appreciation: Where pastoral counselling has helped, the client may wish to express thanks to the helper. The helper also may express his own appreciation of being allowed to share in the thoughts and feelings of the client, if he feels it is appropriate to do so.

Assessment: A useful part of concluding is to assess progress, and what still remains to be done. People sometimes do their own evaluation without prompting, reviewing in what ways they have changed, and what aspects they still wish to work upon in themselves. If such self-assessment is not volunteered, the pastoral counsellor might wish to introduce it at the last meeting, asking what has been helpful and what has not. By doing this he gives a chance to the person to express both positive and negative feelings which may not already have been voiced. If counselling has to end prematurely, the counsellor can suggest areas upon which a person may wish to continue to reflect, while of course supporting any progress that has been made.

Not all endings are as straightforward as those described. Apart from denial or relief, which rule out consideration of the above responses, there are two particular ways in which feelings about endings are obscurely expressed. In chapter 8 the resistance to ending through the return of problems, or the advent of new problems, was mentioned. When a person reports further problems the pastoral counsellor may wonder whether it is indeed right to finish. There can be no hard and fast rules in such situations, although when a contract has been made (as may happen in more formal counselling), and where prior to the approach of the end a client appears to have been progressing well, this re-emergence of difficulties may be seen as an unconscious reaction, a way of saying 'Don't leave me now'. By trying to bring out the feelings of disappointment and anger the counsellor often finds that the breaking through of old problems is only temporary. It is less easy in informal pastoral contacts to use such an approach, although similar 'tapping' of such feelings will again help to make the conclusion more bearable.

Sometimes the reaction will be more openly stated, as in the request for more time. Those counsellors who work to a contract will in most instances gently refuse the request, but at the same time suggest the presence of feelings about stopping. Some clients (more particularly in formal counselling) suggest stopping sooner than agreed, or stay away from the last appointment, or the penultimate one. Since separations evoke sadness, disappointment and anger, some people prefer not to experience them, or not to share such feelings, and so take steps to avoid them. Occasionally a person 'acts out', for instance by letting down someone else important to them, just as he himself feels let down by the counsellor.

The description given of responses to endings is equally applicable to pastoral contact of any regularity, as such pastoral work approaches its conclusion. However, in counselling as such it is more possible to use the responses to endings as ways of understanding the past and present relationships of clients. I conclude, therefore, with some examples of ways in which endings can be handled in more formal counselling. In all these instances the counsellors concerned were following the practice of reminding the client of the impending break (whether temporary or final) at least three weeks before it was due to occur. By doing this the counsellor gives the client a chance to respond directly. Alternatively, having 'sowed the seed' he can listen for any indirect reference to breaks or separations which might be relevant to the break with himself. If he is working to link past and present, outside experiences and those within counselling, he can sometimes relate what is said to the different points of 'the triangle of insight'. Because endings provide such opportunities, a counsellor can also suggest to anyone wishing to terminate the meetings that he comes for three more sessions, to allow the end to be more fully explored. This, incidentally, provides a breathing space at the same time in which the client's decision to leave can be reviewed. The wish to stop might be an impulsive reaction, a sign of some resistance. The three further meetings give time for second thoughts and more considered action.

Let us look then at some examples of the handling of endings and breaks in more formal counselling:

A woman in her twenties, Miss Young, was coming to the end of a job, and had to move to another part of the country to find work. This meant that she would no longer be able to see her minister. About six weeks before she was due to leave she talked about her dependence on her parents when she was a teenager. She would miss them when she moved, even though she was much less dependent upon them now. Indeed she was often irritated by the way they fussed over her. Although she had not normally responded to allusions made by the minister to feelings she might have about him, he took this opportunity to suggest that she might also be concerned at the prospect of not seeing him any more. Miss Young thought for a while, and replied, 'That's funny—as I was coming here today I was thinking about that. It's true, I will miss you, but there is a difference between you and my parents. You don't make demands on me like they do, and you don't force your ideas on me. It will be more natural to say goodbye to you.'

Dr Zenner was a research chemist in his late twenties, seeing a counsellor because he was depressed. This was more acute in relation to his work since he was highly self-critical. As they approached a summer break, when both he and the counsellor were due to take their holidays, Dr Zenner angrily described how he was being pressed by his father about business matters, and yet he was getting no help from him, because father was not prepared to listen when he tried to talk about finance. He felt he was always having to cope with arrangements for other people, who just made him get on with it. His boss had turned a deaf ear to his request for help with his latest project. He expected him to get on with it and did not give him any advice. All this gave the counsellor a lead in for his observation that Dr Zenner probably felt that he did not get all the help he wished for from the counsellor, and that with the summer break coming up he was angry at being left to cope with various decisions on his own. Dr Zenner agreed, and said that when he did not have the counsellor to talk things over with, he worried that his decisions would go wrong and make him more depressed.

My final example is of greater length, and illustrates the context of the use of endings more clearly. It shows how significant the observations can be. Drawing attention to the separation allowed new and important material to emerge, from which fresh insight followed for both the client and the counsellor, even at such a late stage. It illustrates that techniques, whether used in connection with endings or any of the other aspects of the counselling relationship are never used as ends in themselves. They constantly serve a wider purpose, which is the enrichment of the counselling, leading to greater self-awareness. This can come about when sensitive and accurate interventions are made by the counsellor at the right moment:

Mrs Jackson was a writer of short stories which appeared in magazines. Her husband paid little attention to her and the marriage had been short-lived. She now had a new partner whom she was considering marrying. The main problem which she brought to the pastoral counsellor was a meeting with her father which was shortly due to take place, and about which she was feeling very anxious, since she had not seen him for many years. After the initial interview the counsellor suggested that they meet for twenty sessions, ten leading up to the meeting with father, and ten afterwards.

Her family history emerged quite quickly in the first two sessions, which were packed full of information delivered very rapidly. Mrs Jackson's parents had divorced, she said, when she was eleven years old, and she had not seen her father since. She had been told by her mother that one of the reasons for the divorce was that her father had been very mean with money and done little to support the family. This information later turned out to be untrue. Because she spoke in such a rush the counsellor sensed her anxiety, and he wondered aloud in the third session if she felt disappointed when he said that it was time to finish, since she appeared to want to say so much. She denied this, and said how grateful she was to have a time limit, and also a fixed number of sessions. She said she was concerned that otherwise she would come to see him one week with nothing to say and he would then suggest stopping early. She obviously valued the opportunity given to her to talk, but he felt in his own mind that leaving was an issue, and that it might be seen in terms of rejection for not being co-operative. As it turned out rejection was feared on almost the opposite grounds.

The sessions proceeded very well. Mrs Jackson was a thoughtful person who had a lot of insight, and she worked very hard. Nothing untoward occurred until the third session before the last, when she started by suggesting that she felt it was only necessary to meet once more, and that she would not mind missing the last two weeks. The counsellor replied that he thought she wanted to avoid the feelings associated with stopping, and she agreed that she would abide by the original arrangements.

At the penultimate session Mrs Jackson spoke about her parents' marriage in a way which she had not done before. She said that her parents had in fact separated when she was five, and that she remembered wondering why, even at that age. She had been a very high-spirited and excitable little girl, and she thought that it was her exuberance which had made father go away. When she began to live with her mother alone she became subdued and introverted, playing on her own, living in a make-believe world, in which she made up adventures about Robin Hood and Maid Marion. She said she was very anxious to have everything sorted out before her sessions with the counsellor ended, since she did not wish to have unanswered questions in her mind, as there had been when her parents had separated.

The final session was different again. She arrived dressed completely in black—a colour which she did not normally wear—and she announced that she had given up her writing, and she had decided to leave her male friend, of whom she had previously always spoken warmly. She explained that she was not getting enough love from him, and that she did not feel a real woman with him. She expressed anger also that her father had not taken more trouble to see her after her parents' separation. The counsellor felt that she was reacting very strongly to the ending with him, and that giving up her work and her boyfriend was a sign of this. He intervened at several points in the session. He pointed out that she was dressed in black as if for a funeral, and that she seemed to feel rejected by him from the excitement of counselling, where she had so much enjoyed talking to him. The artificial end of counselling was like the abrupt end of her parents' marriage. He felt he was being seen as deserting her and rejecting her as a woman. It was like the feeling which she had had when she was five, that her father rejected her because (as she had thought then) she was too high-spirited and excitable. She seemed to be taking out the anger felt at her father and the counsellor on herself by not working, and on her boyfriend by identifying him with them. All this was an impulsive response to the feelings of rejection which she had over and above the sadness of leaving.

He did not say all this at once, but as the session went on her mood began to change. She described the positive changes that had taken place over the last few months. She expressed her gratitude to the counsellor for allowing her to vent her anger, which she had indeed felt very strongly. A week later she wrote to him, and in her letter she said: 'I thought I would drop you a line to let you know that you were right yet again. I think at our last meeting I was feeling terribly neglected, though up until that time I don't think I ever really appreciated how much my sense of self and sexuality was tied up with sharing my emotions and thoughts. One of the most important things I have learned about myself through our conversations is how much I try to curb my emotional and intellectual enthusiasms and yet it is from them that I receive greatest fulfilment.' She concluded by saying that she was working well again, and was ready to begin facing the implications of her relationships with others.

The conclusion of any pastoral relationship, but in particular of the counselling relationship, contains as much as the rest of the contact for helping a person to understand himself.

The handling of endings makes it easier for counsellor and client to let each other go.

*

I too am aware of having to 'let go' as I finish these pages, and I have yielded to the temptation to conclude, as above, with an example of how effective pastoral counselling can be, given on the one hand a well-motivated and 'hard-working' person, and on the other a counsellor who is able to use the techniques learned in his training sensitively, thus allowing clarification of the complex issues which arise. Many of the shorter examples used in this book also illustrate the successful use to which counselling skills can be put. If there is a paucity of examples which demonstrate inappropriate handling of difficult situations it is because, as one of my own training supervisors put it, 'We teach by our successes, we learn from our mistakes.'

All who embark upon and continue the practice of pastoral counselling will make mistakes, as well as enjoy successes. Training for counselling is an ongoing process. Books can only take you so far. Each new person seen adds to the experience and learning of the pastor, while the sharing of his work in supervised discussion will enable him to learn more fully from his practice.[3] Through the careful use of his own thoughts and feelings, through listening to the 'still, small voice' within himself and in the other, the pastoral counsellor will find that this particular way of being alongside people in need brings emotional, intellectual and spiritual fulfilment.

Recognizing that, in this world at least, there is greater complexity in human emotions and relationships than some religious sentiments acknowledge, and that peace of mind is rarely attained without prior strain and stress, the prayer of the pastor in his counselling ministry might well be taken from the popular hymn 'Dear Lord and Father of Mankind':

> Drop thy still dews of quietness,
> Till all our strivings cease;
> Take from our souls the strain and stress,
> And let our ordered lives confess
> The beauty of thy peace.

Breathe through the heats of our desire
Thy coolness and thy balm;
Let sense be dumb, let flesh retire;
Speak through the earthquake, wind, and fire,
O still small voice of calm!

Notes

1. J. Macquarrie, *The Principles of Christian Theology*. SCM Press 1966 p. 69.
2. This is one of those references which has eluded identification. I would like to acknowledge the source; perhaps someone who reads this and knows the example will enlighten me?
3. 'Supervision — A Professional Necessity', a videotape featuring the author supervising a trainee counsellor is available for hire from the British Association for Counselling Film Library, 37a Sheep Street, Rugby, CV21 3BX (on Umatic and VHS cassettes).

Appendices

APPENDIX A

Practical Exercises for use in Training Groups, Diocesan Courses, Parish Settings, etc.

These exercises have been designed, or developed from others, by Alan Lilley (counsellor at Loughborough University) and myself, and used by us in our training courses. Most of them can be used with three or four people, although the 'feedback' which is recommended at the end of each exercise will be more comprehensive when there are several small groups.

Important note: If this book is used as part of a training course, we suggest that trainees do not read these pages until the completion of the course.

*

1. Large Group Exercise, to introduce group members to each other, and to highlight some of the problems of listening and remembering.

This exercise needs at least eight people, preferably more, in multiples of four. Odd numbers will mean some people acting as observers.

Give each person a sheet of paper, and ask for the following information to be written upon it. In the middle: name. In the four corners: occupation, a significant person in my life other than a member of the immediate family, a significant event in my life, and my aims in learning about counselling. (Other information can be substituted if the leader prefers.) In the spaces around the name write four hobbies or interests. Tell people that the information will be shared, so that anything too personal which they would not wish to be generally known should be omitted.

Split the group into pairs, nominating in each pair an A and a B. The pairs spend fifteen minutes sharing what they have written with each other. At the end of this time collect the papers in, and ask pairs to join in groups of four people. In each four A introduces his partner B to the new pair for four minutes. B is not allowed to say anything, or to correct any misinformation at the end. The new pair may ask questions about B of the speaker, who answers if he knows. This procedure is followed in turn by B introducing A for four minutes, and then the second pair introduce each other.

After sixteen minutes (a timekeeper is essential) A takes A and B takes B and they pair up with another set of As or Bs. The same procedure is followed in the new sets of four, although this time only two minutes is allowed for each introduction. At the end of this period the whole group should discuss the exercise: what did it feel like to have to remember different conversations? What did it feel like to be talked about, or to hear information distorted, etc.? Frequently there is much misinformation passed on, which often occurs in counselling also, when the counsellor is told of a third party by the client. The comment is also often made that we tend to hear what we want to hear, and not what the other wishes us to know.

2. An Exercise in Pairs in Accurate Remembering

Form into pairs, and take it in turns to talk for five minutes to the partner about an agreed subject: e.g. what I did last weekend, or my last holiday. The partner is simply to listen without saying anything, and at the end of five minutes has three minutes to repeat back as much as possible, if possible in the correct order, to the speaker. Now repeat the exercise the other way round.

This exercise asks us to act as human tape-recorders. Given sufficient practice it is possible to retain much of what we hear and observe, and one of the lessons is that the more silent we are, the easier it is to listen and remember. Although a simple exercise, we have found that for some people it is a new experience to be listened to without interruption. The exercise helps focus attention on the other, and not, as in many conversations, upon oneself.

3. Perceiving the less obvious. An exercise in pairs

The previous exercise concentrates upon words and on what is obvious. A tape-recorder can perform as well, if not better, on that level. What no machine can do is to pick up the hidden messages conveyed in tone of voice, and in gesture and posture, and then to interpret them. Listening includes feeling into the mood of the other, as well as observation of non-verbal communication.

Each partner is asked to speak about a factual or fictitious incident, in which one emotion is clearly expressed in the words used, while another, or others, are conveyed through the tone of voice, by gestures, or by remarks which give clues to the listener that all is not as it seems. For example, one speaker may describe a day when everything went wrong, from sleeping through the alarm to missing the train, to losing an important contract, etc., in which frustration may be the obvious feeling, but where anger was also the hidden part of the experience. Or another may pretend to be a woman who has had an obscene 'phone call, of which she talks in an overtly shocked way, swearing revenge on all sex maniacs, but covertly expressing the excitement she felt about it all.

The leader can make up such incidents to hand to each of the partners, or, having given an example, ask them to make up one for themselves. After allowing a few minutes for the speaker to absorb the instructions and role, take it in turns to tell your story to the partner. The listener may this time intervene if he wishes, but where possible listens to the story trying to perceive the underlying feeling(s). The listener checks out this perception with the speaker when he feels it is clear, or at the end of the story.

4. Reflecting back. An exercise in three's or four's.

In each small group the members take it in turns to act as speaker, reflector (counsellor) and as observer(s). The speaker is asked to speak of an occasion, preferably earlier in his life or career, when he first felt he was trying to help someone. This need not be a counselling situation, although it should be one in which there was a personal element involved. The task of the reflector is to assist the speaker to tell the story, and to expand on what it felt like, on any aspects of the story which are not clear, etc. In addition to the aspects of listening already understood from the first two exercises, the reflector should try to observe some of the basic rules in chapter 3.

If there is only one observer, the task is to watch the interaction between the speaker and the reflector, particularly noticing how well the latter facilitates the speaker. When they have finished, comment on the ways the reflector helped or hindered the development of the speaker's story. Eight minutes is a good time to allow for speaker and reflector, and seven minutes for all three to discuss the 'counselling'. If there is a second observer, the task is to make notes of the different feelings generated in the speaker on the original occasion of helping which is spoken about. What gave pleasure or satisfaction to the speaker? What problems did he experience? What caused anxiety or even pain as the helper? When all three (four) members of the group have taken their turn in each role, the groups can come together to share the findings recorded by the second observer, or to discuss the pleasure and pain of helping in the light of their spoken experiences. These will provide a useful lead into chapters 4 and 5.

5. Appropriate and Inappropriate Responses

Working either in small groups, or as a whole class, write down and share with each other appropriate and inappropriate responses on the part of the counsellor to the remarks below, which clients have been known to say. Assess together what makes a good response, and what needs to be avoided by the counsellor in his reply.

e.g. 'I feel like sticking a knife in my wife.'

Inappropriate responses:

'How dreadful!' (expresses shock, moralizing, criticism)
'That sounds very Freudian.' (joke too technical, over-intellectual, being clever)
'What stops you?' (ridicules, dismissive, or even permissive)

More appropriate responses:

'That sounds a frightening feeling to have.'
'What circumstances make you feel like doing that.'
'You sometimes feel you'ld like to get rid of her?'

Now work out both types of response to the following:

a. I can't stand men.
b. You're not helping me.
c. I'm wasting your time. There must be others who are worse off than me.
d. I really think my world is falling apart.
e. Do you like me?
f. The only reason God created women was to provide a good lay.
g. When am I going to get better?

Members of the group may wish to contribute similar remarks they have heard in order to ask others how they would have responded.

6. Role-Play Exercises

Role-plays will be more realistic if the person playing the role of the helper knows little about the client, except what is gradually revealed in response to his interventions and his manner. Avoid reading these scripts through if you wish to use them. Ask a third person to brief the helper and the client. The presence of this third person (or more) as observer(s) allows for fuller feedback at the end of each role-play. The observer can also act as time-keeper. By using a stop-watch, the helper can ask for time out if he feels stuck in the course of the interview. The clock is stopped, the 'client' leaves the room, and returns after the helper has discussed the situation with the observers—who should also be kept uninformed of the client's script. Allowing for time out when necessary, give each helper twenty minutes in all to try and get through to the nub of the problem. When the role play is over, give both helper and client a chance to get out of role, first by saying what they felt but did not express when they played the role, and then by saying what they felt as themselves in playing these roles. Only after de-briefing should the group move on to more general discussion of the role-play.

Role-playing is not amateur dramatics, and there are no prizes for acting. The script is kept to a minimum so that the person playing the client can develop the character, improvising where necessary. He or she should avoid being deliberately obstructive, or putting in other conflicts not mentioned in the script itself. Each person in the training group should be given the chance to play the client, act as the helper, and to be observer.

Role Play A

Brief for the Helper: You are a school teacher, and Hazel is one of your fifth form students, whom you do not know very well. She asks to see you one day, and you meet her in your classroom at lunchtime.

Brief for Hazel: You are a fifth former at a comprehensive school, and you go to see one of your teachers one lunchtime because you are concerned about your best friend who has got into 'bad company' and is 'taking drugs'. Your friend does not know that you are talking about her, so you are very concerned about confidentiality. You are also very concerned about what you can do for her, what help you can advise her to seek. You avoid, with anxiety, or even anger, attempts by your teacher to find out about yourself, saying things like: 'It's my friend. Please help me to help my friend.'

Your friend's boyfriend has just moved into the neighbourhood. His parents are often away at weekends and he invites friends round to parties. Some of them are his cronies from another part of town, though some are also pupils at your school. They smoke 'joints', and your friend has had a smoke and it made her feel 'funny'. There is also pressure for sex, though she has avoided it so far.

In fact this friend you start by talking about is really yourself. If your helper gives you enough confidence you may reveal this. You may respond if it is directly suggested that you are the person, though possibly with a sense of shame and horror at being 'found out'. You are scared of your parents' reaction if they know, of the risk of police raids, and of the pressure for sex.

Role Play B

Brief for the Helper: You are a youth club leader. Mrs Black, whose son John was an active member of your club, has dropped in to tell you how he is getting on at university. He went to university last October, and is now in his second term, although he did not call in to see you himself at Christmas when he was home.

Brief for Mrs Black: You are a housewife of about forty years of age. Your only child John went up to university six months ago. You have called in to tell his old youth club leader how he is getting on — what a good boy he is, how you expect great things of him, how you remember his childhood with pride, how hard he works, how kind he is to you and your husband, etc. Fill this out as much as you wish, with what other people have said about him — his teachers, the vicar, etc.

In fact you are very worried, and if you feel that the helper enables you to reveal your fears, you do so, although remember that you are afraid of facing the idea of 'failure'. Does the helper enable you to acknowledge that things might not be so good after all? If he/she does, you can tell the helper how John's letters got fewer and fewer in the first term, how he was different over Christmas, gave up going to church with you, talked of being fed up, and mentioned others who had left university. You are afraid that he is now going to throw away all those years of education, and leave. Your husband is not really interested, saying that it is up to the boy.

Role Play C

Brief for the Helper: You are a visitor from the church (clerical or lay) and you have heard from the street warden that Mrs Clarke has recently died. You visit Mr Clarke, although you do not know him personally.

Brief for Mr Clarke: You are in your early sixties, recently bereaved, when your wife died after a long illness during which she was at home. You are extremely sad, and speak very slowly. There are many silences if your helper allows them. You speak of how good your wife was to you — 'one of the best'. You were married for 39 years, and if she had lived until Easter you would have celebrated your Ruby Wedding. She had been such a good patient. You retired early to look after her . . . and now this . . . you wish you could join her. Nothing matters any more.

If the visitor from the church makes it possible, you reveal that the last few years have not been so good, because her illness made her very difficult to live with. There were arguments, she was awkward, and often you wished she would die . . . and now she has. The grief is compounded by guilt.

Role Play D

Brief for the Helper: You are the local Methodist minister, visiting one of the families in the congregation, who have recently moved into the area. The minister of their previous church commended them to you, but so far only Mrs Davis and her aged mother have attended. When you call, Mr Davis is the only one who is at home.

Brief for Mr Davis: You are in your middle fifties, and you and your wife have just moved into the area, in order to purchase a house large enough to have your wife's mother to live with you. Since the new minister calls on you, you are careful what you say. There are urgent jobs around the house, which means you cannot spare time for church at present, although you always attended regularly at your old church. It was very good of your wife to offer to have her mother, fulfilling her Christian duty, 'Honour your father and mother, etc'.

In fact since your mother-in-law moved in you have welcomed every opportunity to get away from her incessant talking. You happily drop your wife and her mother off at church and return home for some peace and quiet. You are already aware of the tensions arising between the three of you. If the minister helps you to voice some of your other feelings — anger, resentment, your wish to enjoy life now the children have left home, etc. — you express more of your true self and allow yourself to drop the mask of being a 'good' Christian.

7. An Exercise in Confrontation (see chapter 7)

A good way of practising the art of confronting is to see what it is like to confront yourself. But before that, either try confronting the author, or, if the leader of the training group can accept it, start by confronting him or her about the course. First write down your criticisms in the harshest words and phrases you can think of. Allow yourself to express your anger. Do not be polite.

Now take what you have written and express the same ideas, but in such a way that you could say this to the author, or the group leader, to help him to realize a shortcoming, but not feel too offended at having it pointed out. Your first version helps you get in touch with what you are feeling. The second version will help you phrase those ideas in ways which are not too threatening.

Now try the same exercise upon yourself. Confront yourself over something you do not like about yourself. Write it down in the harshest and most critical way you can. Then take what you have written and phrase it so that you can accept that part of yourself, but at the same time become sufficiently aware of it to want to alter your behaviour or attitudes in some small way.

If you are part of a training group, share your reactions to doing this exercise with another person. You need not share what you have actually written, unless you feel comfortable about doing so.

8. Using Role Playing for Supervision

In small groups take it in turns to role play one of the people you see in your work as a counsellor or pastor. Choose another person to play the counsellor (or your own professional role) and brief them as much as is necessary about your work-setting, and what that person needs to know about your client. Observers can comment as before on the interaction between the counsellor and client. Reflect afterwards not only upon the counselling, but upon the experience of playing your client, and look for new ways in which you now understand that person.

9. Peer Group Supervision

In groups of three or four talk about a piece of helping work or counselling with a particular client. Choose one person to whom you address yourself, although the others present may also wish to share any thoughts they have. Do not be afraid as listeners to put ideas forward, however far fetched they seem. Even if members of the group are inexperienced in counselling, they will have much they can give each other.

When applicable use this method to look at particular aspects of the counselling relationship, as they are studied in this book:

e.g. defences and resistance (chapter 8)
    transference and counter-transference (chapter 9)
    the presence of religious themes or difficult moral issues (chapter 10)
    endings (chapter 11)

10. An Exercise in how others see us (chapter 9)

The aim of this exercise is to help participants become more aware of how they see and are seen by others. It encourages the practice of clear observation, and may help show up blind spots in self-perception and the perception of others. Finally it helps to create an atmosphere of trust, and promotes an ability to give and receive compliments and suggestions.

Form groups of four to six people. In turn focus upon one person at a time in the group. The other members complete the sentence, 'The first thing I notice about you is . . .', describing something very obvious which they see about the person in focus. This may also be the client's first impression of the counsellor. Repeat this for each member of the group.

Return to the first person. The sentence now to be completed is, 'You remind me of . . . who . . .' This time check the similarities or differences between the person in focus, and the one mentioned in this sentence. Again go round the group so that each person in turn is in focus. This part takes longer.

Return to the person originally in focus, and now complete the sentence, 'You make me feel . . .', where the feeling is one evoked in the person making the sentence complete. Check whether this is a feeling which the person in focus would agree he or she conveys, or whether it is saying more about the observer. Repeat round the circle as before.

The fourth sentence to be completed begins, 'I imagine that you might be . . .' which can be completed in any way the person wishes, and again should be checked with the person described to confirm or refine the impression.

Finally each person in the group says what gift (material object or abstract quality) they would like to give each other member of the group. When this is completed the group can discuss what these gifts were saying both about the donor and the recipient.

Discuss the exercise and what has been generally learned from it in the large group.

11. Endings (chapter 11)

At the end of a training course, review your feelings about its ending. Write down on separate pieces of paper what you have liked about the course, and what you have not liked, and put them in different boxes. When all members of the group have completed their papers, draw out one slip from each box and go round, first reading out the anonymous 'dislikes' and finally the anonymous 'likes'.

168 *Still Small Voice*

Acknowledgements:

The first part of Exercise 1 comes from an idea passed on by the Rev. Duane Parker. The rest is our own design.

Exercise 5 is based upon ideas found in L. R. Wolberg's *The Technique of Psychotherapy.* Heinemann 1967, pp. 584-90.

Exercise 7 is based on the confrontation exercise in Gerard Egan's *Exercises in Helping Skills — a Training Manual to Accompany 'The Skilled Helper'.* Brooks Cole Publishing Co., California, (1975), pp. 84-7.

Exercise 10 has been adapted from S11 and S12 in Dona Brandes' and Howard Phillips' *Gamesters' Handbook.* Hutchinson 1978.

Since the other exercises designed by Alan Lilley and myself are more than likely influenced by our own training experiences, we are aware that we may have inadvertently breached copyright. I will be happy to acknowledge any clear use of copyright material if this is pointed out to me.

We are constantly introducing new exercises into our courses, and would be happy to correspond with other trainers who either wish to know of our latest ideas, or to share exercises which they have themselves developed.

The Relationship between Different Therapies and Counselling Methods

Although this book has made use of an analytic model in describing counselling skills, there are different schools of thought within the analytic movement, as well as many other therapies and approaches to counselling which are 'on offer' for training, workshops and for counselling itself. The purpose of this appendix is to review briefly the way in which these therapies have developed from the original work of Freud, and to describe very briefly indeed (scarcely doing justice to any of them) the main emphases of each method. If there have been break-away movements it has been partly because new insights have been insufficiently recognized within the older schools (at least at the time). I shall therefore concentrate upon what seem the positive aspects of the different movements. References for further reading in many of the areas discussed will be found at the end of this appendix.

The development of therapy and counselling spans decades as well as continents. It is possible to draw up a type of genealogical table, and in some instances even an 'apostolic succession'. In order to make most sense of a potentially confusing subject I will divide this history into five sections:

1. Freud and the two early secessions of Adler and Jung.
2. The Neo-Freudians, the second-generation secessions.
3. The newer therapies which mainly develop from American Freudian or neo-Freudian schools.
4. The main-stream development of psychoanalysis in Britain.
5. The independent contributions which have no direct link with psychoanalytic theory, but are loosely linked to behavioural psychology.

1. Freud and the first generation secessions

Freud built his theory and practice upon three basic hypotheses, the importance of the unconscious, of repression and of infantile sexuality. He also developed many of the techniques of understanding resistance, transference and counter-transference. His model of man was initially both mechanistic and biological, with strong emphasis on 'instincts' and impulses.[1]

Freud was an innovator, but he did not take kindly to those whose ideas appeared to challenge his originality, or his firmly held conviction of the centrality of infantile sexuality. Adler was the first to be forced to break from the tight circle in Vienna, and his 'Individual Psychology' has become an independent school of therapy. His ideas have had even greater influence, since they were later taken up by those we call the Neo-Freudians. Adler felt that greater emphasis should be given to the social, family and educational background in development, and key words from his work might be the significance of power, aggression, and feelings of inferiority and superiority.[2]

Jung broke away a few years later. From his work come terms in common use today such as introvert and extravert, and perhaps his greatest insight was the need to balance the conscious and unconscious aspects of personality—thinking and feeling, masculinity and femininity, the individual and the collective unconscious. He has much more to say about the second half of life, where spiritual questions, and the search for wholeness are more significant than the sexual issues in the first half of life. His thinking is often attractive to religious people, although it is certainly not along orthodox Christian lines. Jungian analysts are usually known as 'analytical psychologists'[3].

2. The Neo-Freudians

Adler and Jung both met Freud through the Viennese circle of analysts, although Jung lived and worked all his life in Switzerland. In Berlin another colleague of Freud's, Karl Abraham, was involved in training others who were later forced to leave Berlin by the threat of Nazi persecution, and in so doing split from the main Freudian movement. The main exception in this circle was Melanie Klein who left earlier for England, and whose work is briefly described in section 4.

The four influential therapists I choose from Berlin are Karen Horney, Fromm, Perls and Reich. Since the last two later broke right away they will be mentioned in Section 3. Horney and Fromm went to the United States in the thirties, and together with others already there, such as Harry Stack Sullivan,[4] formed a group now known as the Neo-Freudians. They put much more emphasis on the influence of society and culture in human development although they differ in just how much emphasis they give to these factors. Erich Fromm has shown a profound interest in the relationship between psychoanalysis and other movements such as Marxism, or religion.[5] Karen Horney was perhaps their first feminist, challenging Freud's male-dominated view of mankind, and putting the mother-child relationship in its proper place.[6] Karen Horney's circle in America included such figures as Paul Tillich, and Abraham Maslow, whose 'hierarchy of needs' begins at basic bodily needs and rises to the concept of self-actualization, which includes spiritual needs.[7] Maslow is one of the influences on transpersonal psychology, which has been described as the fourth force in psychology—the others being behaviourism, psychoanalysis and humanistic psychology. Transpersonal psychology is a synthesis of a number of approaches, ancient and modern, eastern and western, and mention of it leads to even briefer mention of the work of Assagioli (psychosynthesis) and Victor Frankl (logotherapy).[8] Tillich carries us into yet another field, the existentialist, where philosophy, theology and psychology intermingle in the work of writers like Kierkegaard, Buber, Jaspers, and even R. D. Laing.

With the list lengthening quickly I must not omit mention of Erik Erikson, who trained under Anna Freud in Vienna and later moved to America. He bridges the Freudians and Neo-Freudians, and is responsible for the useful developmental scheme called 'the Eight Ages of Man', as well as for furthering our understanding of identity, and adolescence in particular.[9]

3. The Newer Therapies from the United States

With the proliferation of therapies which follow we appear to have a modern Tower of Babel, as is suggested by the title of one book, *Psycho-Babble*.[10] We now enter the area known as humanistic psychology, with the founders of diverse therapies coming in the main from Freudian or Neo-Freudian stock.

First we glance back to Berlin in the period between the Wars. Wilhelm Reich trained in Vienna and Berlin, and his fertile mind ranged over many issues—negative transference and the analysis of character traits from physical bearing are still regarded by the analytic schools as major contributions to their work. He differed from Freud in placing particular emphasis on the body itself and on satisfactory orgasm as essential for mental health. Freud was more concerned with wishes and fantasies, Reich with the actual discharge of sexual energy. He therefore points us to the importance of the body, and non-verbal communication through posture and gesture.[11]

His therapy developed into an active working with the body through massage and exercises, and was refined by a follower of his, Alexander Lowen, in the bio-energetic movement.[12] He also influenced therapeutic dance, relaxation, Gestalt therapy and sex therapy. Fritz Perls was analysed by Horney and Reich, and later founded Gestalt therapy, concerned, as the name suggests, with the whole. What is distinctive about Gestalt therapy is its emphasis on the 'here-and-now' and discouragement of reference to the past.[13]

But if 'here-and-now' typifies Gestalt, 'there-and-then' would be more accurate to describe Primal Therapy and the work of Arthur Janov, who took up some of another Freudian colleague's ideas, when he re-instated the importance attached by Otto Rank to the birth trauma.[14] Although Janov's work has some similarities to the primal integration workshops run by Frank Lake in Britain, Frank Lake has moved independently towards the significance of birth and peri-natal experience, using an amalgam of bio-energetics, prayer counselling and primal work.[15] Frank Lake shows an intense interest in theological parallels, and makes a distinctive contribution to pastoral counselling in Britain, although other major pastoral counselling bodies in the United Kingdom tend to follow more traditional lines, using the insights of the analytic and the Rogerian schools.

Many of the therapies described in this section are dramatic and highly charged, with a strong directive element from the therapist. Compared to them Transactional Analysis appears more conventional—it is certainly closer to its Freudian origins than some of the other American therapeutic cults. T.A. was developed by Eric Berne, whose ability to communicate simply and often humorously must have led to his popularity with such books as *Games People Play*.[16] Instead of the Freudian tri-partite division of the mind into id (instincts), ego (central experiencing self) and super-ego (conscience or internalized parents) Berne observes three ego states at work, which he calls Child, Parent and Adult. Even counsellors who do not use T.A. often find these readily understood terms as immediately relevant to their clients in describing inner conflicts and attitudes.

Finally, without here going into the many variations which have come from the West Coast of America, mention must be made of 'co-counselling', originating from Harvey Jackins in Seattle, but with splinter movements in Britain, particularly one led by John Heron of the University of Surrey. Co-counselling differs from many other methods in being a reciprocal form of help offered by two people to each other, although like some others referred to in this section it puts strong emphasis upon catharsis of pent-up feelings.[17]

4. Psycho-analytic development in Britain

The influence of these newer therapies upon counselling in Britain tends to obscure the highly original contribution which analysts from different schools in this country have made to the practice of psychotherapy, and to our understanding of personality development. The study of infancy, of fantasy and of object-relations has added dimensions to pastoral counselling practice lacking in the newer therapies, which on the whole emphasize immediacy rather than deeper understanding.

Analysis in Britain has its own divisions. There are the 'B' group Freudians, for whom Anna, daughter of Freud, is the figurehead; the 'A' group Kleinians, who have followed the work of Melanie Klein, and a middle group who are less partisan and which includes such names as Balint,[18] Bowlby[19] and Winnicott.[20] The Jungians too have made contributions to the British scene, with perhaps Anthony Storr being one of the best-known writers.[21]

Anna Freud has remained close to her father's work, continuing to stress the place of sexuality in neurosis, and the significance of the Oedipal stage around the fourth and fifth year of life. She was one of the pioneers of child analysis in Vienna and London, and puts more emphasis on the part parents have to play in therapy than does Melanie Klein who also practised child analysis. Anna Freud has written about defence mechanisms, and furthered the study of ego-psychology—the formation of the central ego—a somewhat different emphasis from her father's concern with instinctual drives and the id.[22]

Melanie Klein was one of the few of Freud's followers to take up his hypothesis, developed after the First World War, of the Death instinct—although Freud began to give more attention to the problem of aggression at that time, the particular form of his thinking did not receive much favour. Klein, however, developed that thinking and has made a major contribution to our knowledge of primitive rage and envy. She concentrates upon the early weeks and months of life as the breeding ground of the Oedipal problems of the child. She gave impetus to the exploration of internal objects and the power of fantasy. Although Kleinian theory makes an invaluable contribution to our understanding of early human development, the practice itself depends heavily upon transference interpretation, making it less readily adaptable to counselling techniques.[23]

Klein is one of the British school responsible for the development of 'object-relations' theory: moving away from Freud's instinctual theories, problems in development are seen more in terms of relationships. She differs from another major thinker, Fairbairn[24] in placing more emphasis on innate disposition than on external relationships as the contributing factor in the formation of 'internal' objects. ('Objects' is used in the sense of the object of feelings.) She tends to see the basic problem as coping with the fear that hate destroys love, whereas Fairbairn sees the earliest problem as the fear that it is love itself which has destroyed the loved one. He throws light upon the schizoid personality, the withdrawn person who feels and yet fears weakness. 'He would rather feel bad but strong than frightened and weak.'[25] Fairbairn is best studied initially through the writing of Harry Guntrip, a Congregational minister who trained as a psychotherapist under Fairbairn, and has written for the intelligent layman.[26]

In the indigenous British schools we enter a different world from that of the newer therapies imported from the United States. Responsible counselling needs a cogent and intelligible theoretical framework to underpin technique. Understanding of human development, even at these earliest stages of life which have been so well studied by British analysts, not only helps the counsellor understand personality disorder, but also makes a contribution to the work of the pastor and others who work with parents and families in ante- and post-natal care, baptism preparation, etc.

5. Independent Developments

Highly idiosyncratic though many of the therapies are which have so far been mentioned, all have grown out of, even if sometimes in outright opposition to, the Freudian model. The other major force in psychology is behaviourism, which in its turn has engendered different therapeutic approaches.

Carl Rogers, after starting theological training, moved into behavioural psychology, but reacted against it, and against psychoanalysis. His 'client-centred therapy' is therefore more independent of other influences, and it has certainly attracted much support in the counselling field. Rogers' work is most valuable for the development of basic skills and attitudes towards the client, and he seems much more concerned with the therapeutic relationship than with the theory of human personality. His main theory is that given positive esteem in the counsellor/client relationship the client is able to grow and change, and only the client knows how he wishes this to happen. The counsellor's task is one of respecting and understanding what the client is saying now, and is not an analysis of the client's past (except inasmuch as the client wishes to introduce this).[27]

Behaviourism, in which Rogers began his training, is the one major school of psychology and therapy which appears to have little connection with the analytic therapies, and there are still running battles between protagonists on both sides about the effectiveness of their methods. Behavioural psychology builds upon the work of Pavlov, and in particular on the research of two American psychologists, Watson and Skinner. It often forms the major part of university degrees in psychology, where preference is given to the quantifiable study of overt behaviour rather than to the less precise and less easily measured area of unconscious wishes and fears.

Behaviour therapy is favoured by many clinical psychologists and some social workers as a method of treatment, with the claim that its shorter, more focussed methods yield more obvious results than the psychodynamic approach. Relaxation, de-sensitization, operant conditioning, social skills training, etc. are some of the ways in which behavioural therapy is used.[28] It is especially successful with monosymptomatic presentations, such as phobias.

Arguments between behavioural and psychodynamic therapists will no doubt go on, although in recent years there has been greater mutual recognition of the overlap between the two. The therapist's personal approach, and the understanding of transference is now talked about more openly in behavioural schools, while the similarity between de-sensitization and conditioning on the one hand, and repeated working through of problem areas on the other hand, shows one major link in both approaches. Both also recognize that the past influences the present, although behaviourists put more stress on learning theory, and psychodynamic therapists on the power of fantasy. Sex therapy, as demonstrated in the work of Masters and Johnson[29] is a specialized area of behavioural work, although the writing of Helen Kaplan[30] shows how an analyst can draw upon the behavioural approach, while still using psychodynamic techniques when she encounters resistance to graded learning methods.

There are also some 'newer' therapies which owe more to the directive approach of behaviourism than to the more free-floating methods of analytical or Rogerian therapy. They stress reality factors and man's ability to use his will-power to change. Glasser's 'Reality Therapy'[31] believes that if a person behaves responsibly his neurosis will go away, and Ellis' 'Rational-Emotive Therapy'[32] lays down a number of irrational beliefs which are confronted and challenged by the therapist. In these therapies the cognitive problem-solving aspects are given special emphasis, in complete contrast both to the Rogerian belief in non-directiveness, and to the psychodynamic belief in the strength of past experience in determining present behaviour and attitudes.

Mention of one further independent worker leads us into the final area of therapy which has not yet been considered, the use of groups. J. L. Moreno[33] was another emigré from Vienna to the United States, although he was not connected with Freud. He founded psychodrama, in which participants enact dramatically a problem area in their lives, using others to represent key figures in the family or social setting. Moreno's work influenced Kurt Lewin and the development of T-Groups ('T' standing for 'training'), as well as group dynamics generally, systems analysis, encounter groups, Gestalt therapy and family therapy. In fact group work embraces all the diverse forms of the individual therapeutic methods already outlined. In some groups emphasis is upon learning about group process itself, which can then be applied to organizational and institutional settings; in others the group life mirrors the individual dynamics of the group members. Some groups are directive (such as in encounter work where the facilitator introduces different group exercises); others are mainly supportive as each member takes it in turn to work with the therapist (as in Gestalt), while in others the group consultants or therapists are present to interpret—as in the Tavistock and Group Analytic models.[34]

Moreno is only one of those who have influenced the study and work of groups. Others such as Foulkes[35] and Bion[36] have contributed their own models of group life based upon psychoanalytic theory. Social psychologists and sociologists also study group behaviour.

This whistle-stop tour of the therapies can do no more than place the different methods in context, and introduce some of their most positive features. A fuller, more critical account would have also pointed to some of the negative and counter-productive features in many of the therapies. The pastoral counsellor is unlikely to be wedded to any one system, since his clients present in different ways, and differ in their ability to use one approach alone. But the pastoral counsellor needs also to be cautious about eclecticism, which is fast becoming a fashionable term in counselling circles. As a self-description 'eclectic' is in danger of becoming worthless, since what one eclectic believes and practices is not the same as another. The permutations are numberless. Broad-mindedness and flexibility are essential in the pastoral counsellor, but woolliness and purposelessness are only likely to add to the bewilderment of the client, even if the counsellor can tolerate chaotic thinking.

Different therapeutic and counselling methods may appear to lead to the same goal, although it is clear from this account that there are distinct emphases, and any shared goals which do exist are too diffuse to be of any great value. As is the case with the

Appendix B

acquisition of other skills, the apprentice should learn one method until it is sufficiently mastered. When one approach is fully understood, alternative therapies can provide fresh insights, and different strategies. Those who practise counselling need a base from which to move, which acts as a yardstick. Clearly this book has stuck fairly firmly to one such yardstick—had one of the other therapies been chosen as a basic model it might have been very different.

*

References for further study of the therapists and therapies mentioned

General books, describing many of the therapies mentioned:

Brown, J. A. C., *Freud and the Post-Freudians*. Penguin Books 1967.
Guntrip, H., *Personality Structure and Human Interaction*. Hogarth Press 1961.
Harper, R. A., *Psychoanalysis and Psychotherapy—Thirty-six Systems*. Prentice Hall New York, 1959.
Kovel, J., *A Complete Guide to Therapy*. Penguin Books 1978.
Nordby, V. J. and Hall, C. S., *A Guide to Psychologists and their Concepts*. Freeman, San Francisco, 1974.
Proctor, B., *Counselling Shop*. Burnett Books, London, 1978.
Rosen, R. D., *Psycho-Babble*. Wildwood House, London, 1978.

Numbered references:

1. D. Stafford Clark, *What Freud Really Said*. Penguin Books 1977.
   R. S. Lee, *Freud and Christianity*. Penguin Books 1967.
   E. Jones, *The Life and Work of Sigmund Freud*. Penguin Books 1964.
2. A. Adler, *The Practice and Theory of Individual Psychology*. Routledge and Kegan Paul 1929.
3. F. Fordham, *An Introduction to Jung's Psychology*. Penguin Books 1979.
   M. Fordham, *Jungian Psychotherapy*, John Wiley 1978.
   C. G. Jung, *Memories, Dreams and Reflections*. Fontana 1967.
4. H. S. Sullivan, *Conceptions of Modern Psychiatry*. Tavistock 1955.
5. E. Fromm, *Psychoanalysis and Religion*. Yale University Press 1950;
   — —, *The Crisis of Psychoanalysis*. Penguin Books 1973;
   — —, *Fear of Freedom*. Routledge and Kegan Paul 1950.
6. K. Horney, New Ways in Psychoanalysis. Routledge and Kegan Paul 1947.
   — —, *Self-analysis*. Routledge and Kegan Paul 1962.
7. A. Maslow, *Toward a Psychology of Being*. Van Nostrand, USA, 1962.

8. V. Frankl, *The Doctor and the Soul.* Souvenir Press, London, 1969.
9. E. Erikson, *Childhood and Society.* Penguin Books 1965.
10. R. D. Rosen, *Psycho-Babble.* Wildwood House, London, 1978.
11. C. Rycroft, *Reich.* Fontana Books 1971.
12. A. Lowen, *Bio-energetics.* Coventure, London, 1977.
13. F. S. Perls, *Gestalt Therapy.* Dell, New York, 1951.
14. A. Janov, *The Primal Scream.* Putnams, New York, 1970.
15. F. Lake, *Tight Corners in Pastoral Counselling.* Darton Longman and Todd 1981.
16. E. Berne, *Games People Play.* Penguin Books 1964.
    T. Harris, *I'm OK, You're OK.* Pan Books 1973.
17. H. Jackins, *The Human Situation.* National Island Publications, Seattle, 1973.
18. M. Balint, *The Basic Fault.* Tavistock 1968.
19. J. Bowlby, *Child Care and the Growth of Love.* Penguin Books 1972.
20. D. W. Winnicott, *The Child, the Family and the Outside World.* Penguin Books 1973.
    — —, *Playing and Reality.* Penguin Books 1974.
21. A. Storr, *The Integrity of the Personality.* Penguin Books 1972.
    — —, *The Art of Psychotherapy.* Secker and Warburg 1979.
22. A. Freud, *The Ego and Mechanisms of Defence.* Hogarth Press 1937.
    — —, *Normality and Pathology in Childhood.* Penguin Books 1973.
23. H. Segal, *Klein.* Fontana Books 1979.
    M. Klein, *Our Adult World and Other Essays.* Heinemann 1963.
24. W. R. M. Fairbairn, *Psychoanalytic Studies of the Personality,* Routledge and Kegan Paul 1952.
25. H. Guntrip, *Healing the Sick Mind.* Unwin Books 1964, p. 63.
26. See (25) and:
    H. Guntrip, *Psychology for Ministers and Social Workers.* Allen and Unwin 1971.
27. C. Rogers, *On Becoming a Person.* Constable 1974.
    — —, *Client-Centred Therapy.* Houghton Mifflin, Boston, 1951.
28. J. Wolpe, *The Practice of Behaviour Therapy.* Pergamon, Oxford, 1969.
29. W. Masters and V. Johnson, *Human Sexual Inadequacy.* Churchill, London, 1970.
30. H. Kaplan, *The New Sex Therapy.* Penguin Books 1978.
31. W. Glasser, *Reality Therapy.* Harper and Row, New York, 1965.
32. A. Ellis, 'Rational Emotive Psychotherapy', a chapter in *Counselling and Psychotherapy,* ed. by D. S. Arbuckle. McGraw Hill, New York, 1967.
33. I. A. Greenberg, *Psychodrama: Theory and Therapy.* Behavioral Publications, New York, 1974.
34. A. K. Rice, *Learning for Leadership.* Tavistock 1965.
35. S. H. Foulkes and E. J. Anthony, *Group Psychotherapy.* Penguin Books 1967.
36. W. R. Bion, *Experiences in Groups.* Tavistock 1961.

APPENDIX C

Further Reading

Particular therapies and counselling theories are extensively referenced at the end of Appendix B.

Books on (Pastoral) Counselling

The Art of Counselling by Rollo May. Abingdon, Nashville, undated.
Basic Types of Pastoral Counselling by Howard Clinebell. Abingdon, Nashville, 1966.
The Casework Relationship by Felix Biestek. Allen and Unwin 1957.
Counselling by Ethel Venables. National Marriage Guidance Council, Rugby, 1971.
Crisis Counselling by Eugene Kennedy. Gill and Macmillan, Dublin, 1981.
An Introduction to Pastoral Counselling by Kathleen Heasman. Constable 1969.
Introduction to Psychotherapy by D. Brown and J. Pedder. Tavistock 1979.
On Becoming a Counsellor by Eugene Kennedy. Gill and Macmillan, Dublin, 1977.
The Pastor as Counsellor by A. Godin. Gill and Macmillan, Dublin. 1966.
Principles of Pastoral Counselling by R. S. Lee. SPCK 1978.
Psychoanalytic Insight and Relations by I. Salzberger-Wittenberg. Routledge and Kegan Paul 1970.
Psychology for Ministers and Social Workers by Harry Guntrip. Allen and Unwin 1971.
The Skilled Helper by Gerard Egan. Brooks-Cole Publishing Co., USA, 1975.
Tight Corners in Pastoral Counselling by Frank Lake. Darton Longman and Todd 1981.

Books on Specific Life Issues

Adolescent Disturbance and Breakdown by M. Laufer, Penguin Books 1974.
Alcoholism by N. Kessel and H. Walton. Penguin Books 1979.
Bereavement by C. Murray Parkes. Penguin Books 1972.
Childhood and Society by E. Erikson. Penguin Books 1963.
Depression by Jack Dominian. Fontana 1976.
Dying by John Hinton. Penguin Books 1967.
The Growth of Personality by Gordon Lowe. Penguin Books 1972.

179

Human Aggression by Anthony Storr. Penguin Books 1971.
Human Development by Eric Rayner (2nd edn). Allen and Unwin 1978.
The Magic Years by Selma Fraiberg. Methuen 1959.
Marital Breakdown by Jack Dominian. Penguin Books 1968.
On Death and Dying by E. Kubler-Ross. Tavistock, London, 1970.
The Psychology of Human Ageing by D. B. Bromley. Penguin Books 1966.
The Psychology of Moral Behaviour by Derek Wright. Penguin Books 1971.
'Overcoming Common Problems' — a series of books covering many human anxieties and problems, written with the person suffering in mind. Published by Sheldon Press.

Books on Theology, Psychology and Pastoral Care

The Birth and Death of Meaning by Ernest Becker. Penguin Books 1972.
The Christian Healing Ministry by Morris Maddocks. SPCK 1981.
The Church and the Sexual Revolution by Jack Dominian. Darton Longman and Todd, 1971.
Counselling in Religion and Psychiatry by Desmond Pond. OUP 1973.
The Courage to Be by Paul Tillich. Fontana Books 1952.
The Dialogue Between Theology and Psychology, ed. by Peter Homans. University of Chicago Press 1968.
The Dogma of Christ by Erich Fromm. Routledge and Kegan Paul 1963.
The Dynamics of Religion by Bruce Reed. Darton, Longman and Todd 1978.
Faith, Freedom and Conscience by R. Egenter and P. Matussek. Gill and Macmillan, Dublin, 1967.
Freud and Christianity by R. S. Lee. Penguin Books 1967.
Freud and Religious Belief by H. L. Philp. Rockcliff, London, 1956.
God and the Unconscious by Victor White. Fontana Books 1960.
A History of the Cure of Souls by J. T. McNeill. SCM Press 1952.
Life Against Death by Norman O. Brown. Routledge and Kegan Paul 1959.
Pastoral Care in Historical Perspective by W. Clebsch and C. Jaekle. Harper Torchbooks, New York, 1967.
The Pastoral Nature of the Ministry by Frank Wright. SCM Press 1980.
Psychoanalysis and Religion by Erich Fromm. Yale University Press 1967.
Psychology of Religion by Heije Faber. SCM Press 1976.
Psychology, Religion and Healing by Leslie Weatherhead. Hodder and Stoughton 1963.
Theology After Freud by Peter Homans. Bobbs-Merrill, Indianapolis, 1970.
The True Wilderness by Harry Williams. Fontana 1976.
Words of Counsel by Louis Marteau. T. Shand Publications, London, 1978.

Index

182 *Index*